THE BAPTISM
WITH
THE HOLY SPIRIT

and the value of
speaking in tongues today

by
Oral Roberts

Contents

1 Preparing To Be Baptized
With the Holy Ghost

Shortly before His ascension, the Lord Jesus Christ met with His disciples to give them instructions for the future. Those instructions concerned the personal immediate future of each who was present. They also included the future of the Church. They contained God's answer to the dilemma in which the Church finds itself today.

Although the disciples were but instruments of clay, the Lord placed His plans for saving and healing humanity in their hands. First, however, He indicated that they must be prepared. As they gathered around Him, He spoke to them saying that they should not depart from Jerusalem, but wait. When Jesus said "wait" He spoke of reaching a point of *restful expectation*. There was no place for anxiety, dread or fear of the future in Jesus' plans for them then—nor is there for you and me today. *Wait*, He said, *something is ahead. The clouds will lift, the dawn will break, something of value, of great value will come. Prepare yourself for its coming.*

For what was it that He wanted them to wait? "Wait for the promise of the Father . . . which ye have heard of me. For John truly baptized with water; but ye shall be baptized with the Holy Ghost not many days hence" (Acts 1:4, 5). They were to wait in Jerusalem for the Father's promise which is the baptism with the Holy Ghost. Notice that in this passage Jesus spoke of two baptisms, one already experienced and the other future; thus, carefully making it clear that the baptism with the Holy Ghost is not baptism with water but a totally different experience.

Following this initial statement, Jesus made a more detailed explanation as to why He wanted the disciples to wait. "Ye shall receive power," He said, "after that the Holy Ghost is come upon you: and ye shall be witnesses unto me . . ."

(Acts 1:8). He began His instructions by reminding them that even before His crucifixion He had told them that they were to receive the promise of the Father which is the baptism with the Holy Spirit. He had promised that the Holy Spirit would come to fill the void created by His being no longer with them in the flesh, and that in the Spirit He would be even closer to them after His earthly departure. In a real and wonderful way this experience of the Holy Spirit would mean more to them than if Jesus remained physically with them and they continued to see, hear, touch or converse with Him in the flesh. The reason for this was that they would receive power after the Holy Spirit had come upon them. Through this power, Christ would be brought back to them as if He had never left and they would reflect and reproduce Him in all His reality in their world. Through the power inherent in the baptism with the Holy Ghost, they would be alive *inside* and *outside* even as He was. Christ would continue to be the center of their lives. He would do it through the Holy Spirit for, "He [the Holy Spirit] shall testify of me," was the promise of the Lord.

The keynote of the baptism with the Holy Spirit was to be power. This was to be a different kind of power than they had received when they first believed on Him. "As many as received him, to them gave he *power* to become the sons of God" (John 1:12). This is power received through conversion. It is the power of *legal right* or *authority* to become something: in this case, a son or daughter of God. In Acts 1:8, Jesus spoke of a different power. In the Greek, this word used by Jesus is "dunamis" meaning dynamite. "Ye shall receive power, after that the Holy Ghost is come upon you: and ye shall be witnesses unto me both in Jerusalem, and in all Judæa, and in Samaria, and unto the uttermost part of the earth." This particular kind of power—the power of enablement—is present in some degree in both conversion and sanctification. Its fullness, however, is received after the baptism with the Holy Ghost has become an integral part of one's life and one continues to walk in the Spirit. It is a power that enables one to become like Jesus in a dimension that is not possible before receiving the Holy Ghost. First, it is an explosive power to witness—not of something but of a Person, the Lord Jesus Christ. Jesus said, "Ye shall be witnesses of ME." Second, it is a power to be a witness *wherever* one is. He doesn't have to "go" somewhere in order to witness— he *is a witness* anywhere he is.

The power of enablement is what those disciples wanted. Christ's physical presence with them had generated this kind of power. At times they had healed the sick, cast out devils, won men to their Lord, and done His great works. But this power was a fleeting experience in their lives. They had not been able to maintain the dynamics of it. Then came the promise of the Lord, "Ye shall receive power, after that the Holy Ghost is come upon you." They were thrilled to learn that they could have this power every day of their lives; and through it, they would be linked to Jesus and Jesus to them in a way that they would be made His true witnesses at all times and in all places where they happened to be. It welded them together like pieces of steel under fire. Jesus was soon to leave. They were to be left alone in the world; yet not alone, because of the coming of the Holy Spirit.

The disciples became so exhilarated with this thought that when Jesus was ready to ascend they were standing on the "tiptoe of expectation." With eager faces and happy hearts, they returned to Jerusalem where they entered an upper room and remained, looking forward to the glorious hour when they would be baptized with the Holy Ghost and fire.

There is no question but that they gained a new insight into their future as they began to understand what the Holy Spirit would do in them and through them. It filled them with anticipation. It is when understanding dawns upon us today that we too enter into a joyful restfulness in Him and look upon the future with a new optimism and hope. This is a real world in which we live. We are faced with the same problems that they faced when they were being instructed by Jesus to wait for the promise of the Holy Ghost. In some ways the problems we face are more severe. Jesus is putting His plans of saving and healing mankind at this critical stage in history into our hands. The enabling power that will make us explosive witnesses of Christ is the very same power that is inherent in the baptism with the Holy Ghost. Entering into this power is as imperative for us as it was for them. We can accomplish through the power of the Spirit the same things they did. When we understand this, the clouds over us will lift and the dawn will break. We will look upon our task of meeting the needs of people with pure joy for we know we have the power through the Holy Ghost to meet those needs.

Some have been baptized with the Holy Ghost without understanding what they have. I was one of them. Understanding has to come sooner or later or the power that is in the experience of the baptism with the Holy Ghost will either fade away, be misused, or will never be fully released. Prior to 1947, I was in dire need of more understanding of what I actually had. I discovered that receiving the Holy Ghost in His fullness does not mean that one will automatically use the power to become a witness of Jesus Christ. Understanding and obeying is the key. To me the key verse in understanding the power of the Holy Spirit is Acts 1:8: "Ye shall receive power, after that the Holy Ghost is come upon you: and ye shall be witnesses unto me."

Let us look again at the meanings which that verse holds for us.

UNDERSTANDING THE POWER OF THE SPIRIT

First, ye shall receive power. Power has always characterized the ministry of Christ and Christianity. It is the only religion in the world that carries with it the power of its founder to deliver people from sin, disease, demons and fear. Christianity is a healing religion, a religion of a new birth, a religion of sanctification and personal purity, a religion of power against the forces of evil in the world. Jesus spoke of all power in heaven and in earth being given to Him. (Matthew 28:18.) He said that He gives this power unto His followers; and through it they are to heal the sick, including all manner of sickness and disease; and through it they are to have the ability to cast out demons. (Luke 10:19.)

This same power was demonstrated in the first century by men and women like you and me. Paul, many years after Pentecost, spoke of the needs of the people being met "through the power and demonstration of the Spirit." The writer of Acts says that "God wrought special miracles by the hands of Paul." Miracles and healings were common in the ministry of men like Philip and Peter and John. James indicated in his letter to the "twelve tribes scattered abroad" that healing was and should continue to be present in the ministry of the Church. Paul also spoke of the gospel as being "the power of God" (Romans 1:16). It is the power of God because it is inbreathed by the Holy Ghost. The men who wrote the Bible were inspired by the Holy Ghost. And when those Spirit-anointed words were spoken by a Spirit-baptized witness they became, "the power of God."

This power of the Holy Ghost is more explosive than the power experienced in salvation. The reference in John 1:12 to the power through which one becomes a son or daughter of God denotes right, authority. The word "power" in Acts 1:8 denotes dynamite, explosive power, the power of enablement. Power in John 1:12 is the power to become. Power in Acts 1:8 is not only *to become*, but *to do* and *to be* like Jesus with the *force of an explosion*.

Since the Lord Jesus Christ told the disciples that He would come back to them after His earthly departure, and would live in them through the power of the Holy Ghost; and, since that same power is available to all believers today, it is also true that we may fellowship and experience the presence of Jesus Christ as though He had never left. His person in power, personality, compassion, love, meekness, gentleness, wisdom, knowledge, faith, healing, miracles, discernment, prophetic utterances—may be present in us in the same dimension as it was in His disciples after they received the baptism with the Holy Ghost.

It was in 1947 that I began to understand this. It was the turning point in my life. I was pleading with God to enable me to begin the ministry of healing. I asked Him to let me see Jesus in the flesh as the Apostles had seen Him. I sensed that my time to start the healing ministry was at hand. I felt the need of power, that dynamite that Jesus spoke of in Acts 1:8. In those days I was studying the four Gospels and the Book of Acts, virtually day and night. I had almost memorized the Book of Acts, because it is a written record of what the Holy Ghost can do in the lives of dedicated men and women. Simple ordinary people, filled with the Holy Ghost, went forth with enabling power to be like Jesus and to do the things that Jesus did and to do them in such a way that people "took knowledge of them that they had been with Jesus."

I had a vision of doing this. A *vision* that grew in me day after day. It became the inspiration of my life. It was during those days that He reminded me that I had received the baptism with the Holy Ghost in 1935. He asked me if I knew what I had. When I replied in all honesty that I did not, He reminded me that having the Holy Ghost was like having Jesus physically by my side; and, therefore, I could go forth and take His healing power to my generation.

It was then that I began to see that the word "power" in the context of Acts 1:8, as well as in the entire Book of Acts, was the same power that was in me through the Holy Ghost. Power! Enabling power! The spiritual dynamite within me that would take Jesus and explosively release Him to the minds and souls of the people of my day! I thought my heart would burst as I contemplated the future. I felt I could go forth with this understanding and Christ in me would awaken thousands to the reality of God in both His saving and healing power.

A Witness of Jesus

I think the clearest idea that I understood in those beginning days of 1947 was that the baptism with the Holy Ghost gave me the power that made me a witness of Jesus and that my mission field is wherever I am at any given moment. This understanding has continued to grow in me. Jesus as a person lives in me in a new and greater way. Although I have not seen Him physically as the disciples did, yet I feel I have seen Him. I have seen Him and felt Him and known Him through the power of the Holy Ghost. I honestly believe He is as real to me as He was to them.

Second, "ye shall be witnesses unto me." One of the sad things today is the terrible division there is in Christianity. The division is caused partly by Christians who have become witnesses to minor values instead of witnesses of the dynamic *person* of Jesus Christ. This is partially true because of the rise of theological systems in which one religious group feels that its reason for being is to emphasize one or two values that another group has neglected. The inevitable result of this type of emphasis is that Christians become absorbed in the ideas that are peculiar to themselves rather than active witnesses of Jesus Christ.

This kind of witness is illustrated by the story of a college girl who had told her religious counselor that even though she had been in school for just a few weeks she had already witnessed to every girl in her wing of the dorm. The counselor asked her what she had said in her witness. The girl replied, "I told them flatly that I don't smoke; I don't drink; I don't play cards; I don't dance; I am different; I am a Christian." The counselor countered, "And now, I suppose, every girl in your dorm wants to be like you." The girl hesitated a moment, and then defended herself with the statement, "At least they know where I stand." But they had not learned a thing about the wonderful Christ—at least, not at that time, for it must be admitted that the girl did finally learn her lesson, and learned it so well that she desired to make others want to be, not like her, but like her Lord Jesus Christ.

This is not to infer that the things that such people stand for are not part of the truth. They are. The trouble is that anyone who tries to witness to the truth can never do it completely. This is because the great religious truth is a person, that person is Christ; and only as we put our emphasis upon Him can we fully bring truth to the world. Unless we witness to Christ, we can never witness to anything but to a part of the truth. When we are witnesses of Him, we witness not only to the truth but to the *way* and to the *life*. Christ is more than truth. He said, "I am the *way*, the *truth* and the *life*." One can witness to the truth and yet not know the *way* to live for God or to have the *life* of Jesus Christ in him.

Jesus came not to talk about truth, He is The Truth. He came not to show us the way, He is The Way. He came not to talk about life, He is Life. Christianity is more than a course in right thinking or emphasizing periphery truths or giving up certain habits or even going to some particular place to worship. . . . Christianity is Jesus Christ of Nazareth, and knowing Him is the way, the truth and the life. He is the living embodiment of all that is good, of all that is truth, of all that is alive, and of all that is eternal. By being witnesses of Him, we will also be witnesses of truth. We will emphasize certain truths. We will worship God in His house. But we will not confine or limit ourselves to some part of the truth or to worshiping in some particular place only. We have Him in us and with us wherever we are; thus, we are living witnesses of Him here and now.

In the infancy of the Church, Jesus Christ, our Saviour, was telling all His followers—including you and me—that through the baptism with the Holy Ghost they are given enabling power to be witnesses to Him, the Person. He called the Church His Body. That Body is not to be distinct from Him who is the head of the Body. Everything that He is must be reproduced by His Body and given to mankind. If His Body, the Church, spends its time emphasizing minor *values* rather than preaching "Jesus Christ and Him crucified," it misses the mark. When the Church helps bring all that He is to all that we are not, then it is His living Body.

Christianity, the gospel, the Christian experience, or the Christian walk, is really a "person." This person is the brightness of God's glory and the express image of His person. This is borne out in the dialogue between Philip and Jesus. Philip said, "Shew us the Father and it sufficeth us." Jesus replied, "He that hath seen me hath seen the Father" (John 14:8, 9). What Jesus is saying to me is: "Oral, if you want to see God, look at Me. I am what God is like. I am a person and you can become this kind of person." Someone has pointed out that "Christian" means *little Christ*.

Being filled with the Holy Ghost provides power, enabling us to reflect and reproduce Jesus Christ in our generation so that He meets the needs of people in our day. Our reason for being is to be witnesses unto Him. People will take knowledge of us that we too have been with Jesus.

Since 1947, as I have preached the gospel of deliverance to multitudes, this truth has been growing inside me until today it is all-absorbing. I have begun to understand that Jesus intends for us both *to bear witness* of Him and *to be witnesses*. The sun is a ball of fire; the light that blesses the earth bears witness of its reality. Christ is in us, and through us the Holy Spirit radiates the life and character of Jesus. Like a ball of fire, we are His witnesses—the radiant life we live bears witness of the reality of Christ in us. The Holy Spirit animates our witness, making the light of truth shine more brightly. To be a witness means a personal encounter with Christ; a day-by-day experience of Christ; a meaningful reflection of His being in us, and a constant outflowing of His Spirit through us to touch other lives for His glory.

It isn't easy for a person to give himself to another person. This is true in marriage as well as in Christianity. We tend to build everything around self. So often the personal ego gets in the way of the Spirit's purpose. We frustrate His purpose by not wholly cooperating with Him so that He can make us like Jesus and release Jesus in and through us. Jesus teaches us that as the Holy Spirit directs our lives we will have explosive power to share Him with people throughout the world.

Jesus Christ Is the Baptizer

Everything in Christianity should reflect Christ as its center. The chief purpose of the Holy Ghost is to testify of Jesus. *Jesus Himself is the baptizer*. John the Baptist said, "I indeed baptize you with water unto repentance: but he that cometh after me is mightier than I, whose shoes I am not worthy to bear: he shall baptize you with the Holy Ghost, and with fire" (Matthew 3:11).

When Jesus has baptized you with the Holy Ghost, He has given you a power to glorify Him and to cause Him to stand forth in your life in a pronounced way. The Holy Ghost seeks to manifest Christ through your life and to set in motion a way of deliverance of people from the power of Satan.

Notice that Jesus stated that this power of enablement is to be used in relation to Himself—"Ye shall be witnesses of me." This means we are to become *Jesus people*. I used to wonder why so many people coming into our crusades would from time to time find themselves in tears while listening to the preaching, or watching the invitation to the unsaved, or observing the prayers for the healing of the sick. I have asked different people why they cried so much and they told me that it is because they felt Jesus was present. It is true that when people feel Jesus they are softened. He makes a direct impression upon their being.

At one time I thought that if I was to be a witness of Jesus unto the uttermost part of the earth, I would have to become a foreign missionary. This is because I had come up under a Christian concept which so structured Christian witnessing. I also had the idea the best place for witnessing in a community was in the church service within the sanctuary of the church. I continue to believe this is a valuable part of our witness. But I now know that one who is filled with the Spirit is a missionary wherever he is. He doesn't have to go anywhere to be a witness. He is a witness at all times. The place where he is, is his mission field. If he is in a foreign land, he is a witness. If he is at his own house, he is a witness there. If he is in the sanctuary of his church, he is a witness of Jesus Christ there. When the Christian is with the leader of his country, or the leader of his community, or his wife, or his children, or the people with whom he works at his job or profession, he is a witness of Jesus Christ.

Power to be a witness of Jesus Christ is the basic purpose of the baptism with the Holy Ghost. *This Baptism provides an inner power that becomes an outward force to bring the reality of Christ to others. To help release this power, the Holy Ghost gives the believer a new tongue. This is one of the most revolutionary experiences that can happen to a believer.*

2 Your New Tongue of Prayer and Giving Thanks to God

In Mark 16:15-20, we are given several evidences of vital Christian experience. They were given by Jesus possibly near the time that He gave us Acts 1:8. The statement starts with the Great Commission to go into all the world and to preach the gospel to every creature and to win souls; that is, to be a witness for Jesus Christ wherever one is in the world. Then Jesus said, "These signs shall follow them that believe. . . ." These signs are five in number: (1) Casting out devils. (2) Speaking with new tongues. (3) Taking up serpents (enemies). (4) Drinking some deadly thing without being hurt by it (accidental). (5) Laying hands upon the sick that they may recover. The chapter ends with these words, "And they went forth, and preached every where, the Lord working with them, and confirming the words with signs following."

All five evidences or signs followed the believing members of the Early Church. They cast out demons. The records of Acts and of the Early Church fathers indicate that they continued to speak with new tongues. They took up serpents.

Taking up serpents does not refer to handling snakes. This was an idiom of the East that referred to enemies. It means what Jesus referred to in Luke 10:19, "Behold, I give unto you power to tread on serpents and scorpions, and over all the power of the ENEMY: and nothing shall by any means hurt you." This was power enabling them to overcome their enemies who would attempt to impede their spiritual progress, or would seek to prevent their being witnesses of the Lord Jesus Christ.

They were made immune or protected from being hurt by contaminated food or drink. Traveling in those days was hazardous in many ways, not the least of which was poor sanitation, bad water and food. Yet there was the sign of promised power of protection even when one unwittingly drank some deadly thing. Most of us who travel widely for the gospel appreciate this particular promise very much. We eat and sleep in all kinds of places, good and bad. Faith in the Lord to keep this promise has given me protection during the years of ministering to the sick. God has never allowed one of the diseases of the people for whom I have prayed to come upon me. I thank God for this.

They prayed for the sick and the sick recovered. That the practice continued in the Church is evidenced by the exhortation of James, "Is any sick among you? let him call for the elders of the church; and let them pray over him . . . and the prayer of faith shall save the sick, and the Lord shall raise him up."

The Gifts Today

In our day there has been a renewed interest in the exercise of all of these gifts. Much is being written, and earnest inquiry is being made in all of these fields. The healing ministry is an example. People of many denominations have discovered the present validity of the promise: "They shall lay hands on the sick, and they shall recover" (Mark 16:18). The healing ministry is reaching new heights of acceptance in our day.

Only recently, a pastor brought his board of elders and asked me to share the healing ministry with them. They wanted to start laying hands upon the sick in their church. Although this particular denomination had not stressed healing for the sick in the past, this pastor and board of elders were hungry for healing to become a part of their Christian witness. It was a pleasure to share with them.

Of particular concern in the twentieth century Church is the exercise of "tongues."

Tongues

"They shall speak with new tongues," is one of the evidences which Jesus promised of vital Christian experience.

Jesus had carefully prepared His disciples to be ready to receive the Holy Spirit. To the very last minutes before His ascension, He was sharing with them what they would receive and how they would be witnesses unto their world. He talked about a new kind of power coming upon them after they received. Doubtless He spoke of the new tongue that was to be given them. It is evident that He mentioned this tongue prior to their receiving the Holy Ghost, because of their ready acceptance of it. "And they were all filled with the Holy Ghost, and began to speak with other tongues, as the Spirit gave them utterance" (Acts 2:4).

Tongues were not to be some freakish experience that would be present one moment and gone the next. It was actually a *point of power release* in those early disciples. Much later Paul said, "I thank my God, I speak with tongues more than ye all" and, "I would that ye all spake with tongues" (1 Corinthians 14:5, 18). Today we are finding that it is a source of power release in us, too.

It is important to point out the different names that were given to this experience of receiving the Holy Ghost in His fullness. Jesus called it a coming upon (Acts 1:8) and a baptism with the Holy Ghost (Acts 1:5). When the 120 received this experience, it was described as being "filled with the Holy Ghost" (Acts 2:4). In explaining it to the multitude who came to see and hear, Peter called it a "gift of the Holy Ghost" (Acts 2:38). It is a baptism, a coming upon, a filling and a gift. These terms are synonymous when applied to receiving the fullness of the Holy Ghost.

The Book of Acts clearly points out that speaking in tongues was a practice of those who received the fullness of the Holy Spirit. It was a meaningful part of Paul's experience. We are not told when Paul began to speak in new tongues, although it is implied that he began when he received the gift of the Holy Ghost by the laying on of hands by Ananias in Damascus. It is irrelevant to know *when* Paul began. We know that he did and, therefore, he had to start some time. We know further that one can speak in tongues only through the power of the Holy Ghost. Speaking in tongues was such a normal experience in Paul's life that he made many definite statements concerning speaking in tongues. These in 1 Corinthians 14 include:

"I would that ye all spake with tongues" (verse 5). "He that speaketh in an unknown tongue speaketh not unto men, but unto God" (2). "If I pray in an unknown tongue, my spirit prayeth" (14). "I thank my God, I speak with tongues more than ye all" (18). "Forbid not to speak with tongues" (39).

It is indicated both in the Book of Acts and in Paul's teaching that speaking in tongues has a fourfold function in the believer's life and witness. First, he speaks in tongues as a part of his private devotions to God. Second, for his personal edification and release. Third, to edify the Body of Christ. Fourth, as a sign to unbelievers.

Yet, the questions continue to arise: Just how does tongues play a vital part? Why did God link tongues to the baptism with the Holy Ghost? *What is the value* to speaking in tongues?

Values of Tongues

As we study the second chapter of Acts, we sense that the 120 men and women who received the baptism with the Holy Ghost on the Day of Pentecost found release while speaking in tongues. Those that heard them and understood said, "We do hear them speak the wonderful works of God." It is evident that something which was pent-up in them was released while they were speaking with tongues. There has been conjecture that the 120 were attempting to preach the gospel to the foreign Jews gathered there that day. We now know that is not according to the facts. When it came time to preach, Peter did that in his own normal tongue. (Acts 2:14.) The group did not speak in tongues, at least not aloud, during the time Peter was preaching. Paul confirmed this later by saying that he had rather speak five words in his own tongue when he was preaching or teaching than ten thousand in a tongue that was unknown. (1 Corinthians 14:19.) Paul also said that when one speaks in tongues "he is not speaking to men but to God." We know then that their speaking in tongues on the Day of Pentecost was not to men, although the crowd was able to hear and understand a large part of what they were saying.

There was an effect upon the crowd. The effect was just as great upon the disciples for they were being edified.

There is a valid and valuable place for speaking in tongues in the believer's life. This is not during the time that the Word of God is being taught or preached to people. Standing above everything else is God's Word and the preaching and teaching of the gospel. Paul tells us that faith comes by hearing, and hearing by the Word of God. (Romans 10:17.) He also tells us that by the foolishness of preaching God saves men. (1 Corinthians 1:21.) Not foolish preaching, but the foolishness of it. When the Word of God, which is already anointed, is preached or taught by one who is anointed by the Holy Ghost, it is power to save people's lives.

By the same token, just because they did not speak in their new tongue when Peter was preaching or when someone else was preaching in New Testament days does not mean that tongues do not have a deep purpose and meaningfulness to each believer. There is, first of all, the tongue of evidence, or the tongue one immediately speaks in when he is filled with the Holy Ghost as an evidence that he is filled. Peter emphasized this when the Holy Spirit fell on the Gentile Christians at Caesarea. The evidence was, "For they heard them speak with tongues, and magnify God" (Acts 10:46). This is how the Jewish brethren in Jerusalem knew the Gentiles had received. (Acts 11:17, 18.) It was a revolutionary evidence, a divine expression, a new tongue spoken by the natural speech organ, but prompted by the power of the indwelling Spirit. Thereafter the believers had power to speak in this tongue as the Spirit gave them utterance. (1 Corinthians 14:15.)

The new tongues is not only evidence that one has been filled with the Holy Spirit, it is a sign to unbelievers as well. It was a sign to the unbelievers on the Day of Pentecost.

Foot note

Paul called tongues a sign to them that believe not. This is certainly true today.

The Holy Spirit has manifested a tongue through me to unbelievers on several occasions. On two occasions the Spirit's speaking through me was used to bring conviction and faith to the hearts of Jewish men—one was a college professor, the other a businessman. The professor was a converted Jew, but did not believe in speaking in tongues. The other believed in God, but not in Jesus Christ. They were both unlearned concerning the baptism with the Holy Ghost. The professor and I had spent several hours discussing the Holy Ghost as we studied the fourteenth chapter of First Corinthians together. When he was ready to leave, we all joined hands and prayed together. While praying, the Holy Spirit welled up in me and I began to pray in tongues. Later he told Fred Waugh —one of the Oral Roberts University regents who had been with us—that he had recognized some of the words connected with Hebrew chants with which he had been familiar while growing up in the synagogue. Like an arrow, the reality of speaking in tongues entered his heart and he became eager to receive. Within two months he had received this experience. He received while in the home of Fred; immediately receiving and speaking in the Spirit. He said to Fred, "Wasn't that a sweet filling?" Today, he is experiencing a new aliveness in Christ. He finds his witness for Christ is far more effective.

The other Jewish man was present in one of the seminars at our School of Evangelism. He had been brought there by one of our ORU regents. During one of the sessions, I saw that he was under heavy conviction by the Spirit. I was led to speak to him, and instantly I began praying with him in the Spirit. As I was praying, he interrupted me and told me what I was saying in Hebrew. It seems that I was talking to God about his soul and giving praise. The man was profoundly moved when he discovered that I did not speak Hebrew except under the power of the Spirit. This truly was a sign to him from God.

To those believers—whom the Holy Spirit enables to speak

in a new tongue daily in private devotions—it is more than *evidence* and more than a *sign* to unbelievers. It is a *personal edification*. We are edified through it. We are indebted to Paul for making this clear to us. In fact, we owe Paul a great deal for taking time with the Corinthian believers to explain what tongues are, their purpose and function. He does this in the twelfth, thirteenth and fourteenth chapters of First Corinthians, and especially in the fourteenth.

One cannot speak in two earthly languages, simultaneously. The same is true when we pray in the heavenly language. When one uses his new tongue through the Spirit's utterance, he cannot speak in his own normal tongue at the same time. Paul gives us the sense of this in 1 Corinthians 14:14: "For if I pray in an unknown tongue, my spirit prayeth, but my understanding is unfruitful." Paul indicates here that when one prays in tongues it is his spirit praying and not just his mind. His intellect relinquishes active control of the speech centers for a moment. It is centered on Christ. And it stands by as an observer, released so that it can give undivided attention, while the spirit, or the inner being of the believer takes over. Paul continues, "What is it then? I will pray with the spirit [in tongues], and I will pray with the understanding [my intellect] also: I will sing with the spirit [in tongues], and I will sing with the understanding [by my intellect] also" (1 Corinthians 14:15).

Paul seems to indicate that when a believer speaks in tongues he is either praying or singing or giving thanks to God with his spirit rather than with his intellect. This is in harmony with Paul's explanation in 1 Corinthians 14:2, "For he that speaketh in an unknown tongue speaketh not unto men, but unto God." Tongues become the vehicle of the believer's spirit through which he, under the promptings of the Holy Spirit, talks to God in a manner that he cannot through his mind or intellect. If one prays through his intellect, his mind creates the speech patterns and words. When one prays through his spirit, it is his spirit in cooperation with the Holy Spirit that forms the words of a new language through which the deepest feelings of the inner being are expressed to God.

Paul says in the same verse, ". . . howbeit in the Spirit he speaketh." The word, *Spirit* should be capitalized since it refers not to the human spirit, as Paul does in verses fourteen and fifteen, but to the Holy Spirit.

When one is praying "in the Spirit," he is praying or speaking in tongues. Paul uses this term again in Ephesians 6:18, and refers to it as a part of the whole armor of God which the believer is to put on to help him stand successfully against all the wiles of the devil. "Praying always with all prayer and supplication IN THE SPIRIT." Here again Paul links speaking in tongues with prayer and supplication, pointing out that our new tongue is devotional, a tongue of prayer and praise TO GOD.

You can begin to see how meaningful tongues are in the believer's daily life of communication with God. Many Christians find themselves inadequate in prayer. Recently I was introduced to a certain man, and his remark was, "Mr. Roberts, I am so pleased to meet you. I have been wanting to ask you a question for a long time. I find it most difficult to pray. I am a Christian, I love God, and I am eager to serve God. Just last Sunday, I was asked to pray in our Sunday-school class and I simply could not find the words. I was frightened and confused. Please tell me how to pray." I shared with him that prayer, to be successful, must come from both the mind and the Spirit. As Paul indicated, it is praying in tongues AND it is praying with the understanding.

There are many people who have found that as they pray much in the Spirit in their private devotions, listening to the voice of the Lord in the heart as they pray, the Spirit gives them liberty and teaches them the things they should pray about with the understanding when they pray in public.

There are actually two ways to pray. One is when the mind in harmony with one's inner being speaks to God; the mind forming the thoughts and words. This is often successful. Just as often, it is not successful. The mind is sometimes able to reach into the inner depths of our spirit, sometimes it is not. The other way is through tongues. Your spirit in reciprocity with the Holy Ghost seeks out the longings and needs of your inner being and expresses them in a new tongue which flows through your normal speech organs to God. I find that praying in both ways helps me to pray more effectively and successfully.

3 It Is Like a River Flowing

In John 7:38, Jesus compared the baptism with the Holy Ghost to a river flowing out of the believer's innermost being. "Jesus stood and cried, saying, If any man thirst, let him come unto me, and drink. He that believeth on me, as the scripture hath said, out of his belly shall flow rivers of living water. (But this spake he of the Spirit, which they that believe on him should receive: for the Holy Ghost was not yet given; because that Jesus was not yet glorified.)" Remember in Acts 1:8 we are told that Jesus said we would receive power after that the Holy Ghost should come upon us. Here in John 7 He says the same thing but in another way. He refers to the Holy Ghost as flowing "out of your belly." The language, of course, is figurative. The Greek word for "belly" literally means *body cavity*. Figuratively it means *heart*. Subjectively it applies to the pit of the stomach where certain tensions or great emotions are felt.

Paul also spoke of an outflowing of the Holy Spirit from the life of the believer. He spoke of it as prayer in an unknown tongue. And in talking about it, he used the word *spirit*, saying, "If I pray in an unknown tongue, my spirit prayeth" (1 Corinthians 14:14).

Were not Jesus and Paul referring to the same thing? Without trying to locate spirit or belly anatomically, can it not be said that out of the innermost being the Spirit pours forth power, and out of the innermost being also comes forth prayer in tongues?

In another instance Jesus used still another word which seems to be related to the human "spirit." He spoke of the *heart*, saying, "Out of the abundance of the heart the mouth speaketh" (Matthew 12:34). He pictured it as a storehouse where treasure is stored, and said that a good man stores good

25

treasure there and an evil man stores evil treasure there. And He pictured those things as being poured forth in speech, saying, "A good man out of the good treasure of his heart bringeth forth good things: and an evil man out of the evil treasure bringeth forth evil things" (Matthew 12:35).

This picture of the inner man gives significance to the subjective use of the word "belly." Good and evil are both emotion-creating states, and the nerve center in the pit of the stomach—down into what Jesus referred to as our belly —responds to what is going on in the inner being. In the innermost being are many things of which the conscious mind is only partially aware. There are hidden the deep yearnings and longings of the heart; there are the joys and sorrows and fears; there are the good and evil treasures of which Jesus spoke. And when we respond to them, whether we are filled with joy or fear, whatever our deep needs may be, we seem to feel it first in the pit of our stomach.

It is significant that it is in the believer's innermost being that the desire to speak to God in tongues originates. In our deepest self, where our needs really are, the Holy Spirit floods up like a mighty river and starts flowing upward toward God. Our objective thinking processes slip into the background for a few moments; and, out of our heart, or spirit, we begin to speak to God and as it comes over our tongue, it becomes *a new tongue* whereby our spirit speaks to God and is edified and released.

A Dialogue

Dr. William S. Reed, prominent physician and surgeon, and an Episcopalian, recently served with us on the faculty of one of the seminars of our School of Evangelism at the Oral Roberts University in Tulsa. Dr. Reed is filled with the Holy Ghost and speaks in tongues daily to God. The morning I was giving this message in the Laymen's Seminar, I asked Dr. Reed to come to the platform and give us from his viewpoint some of the meanings of Jesus' statement "out of your belly shall flow rivers of living water" as it might apply to speaking in tongues. He responded with a subjective approach to the word "belly."

Here, in essence, is part of the dialogue from the tape:

Reverend Roberts: "Now, how would you say it, Dr. Reed? You speak with tongues like we do."

Dr. Reed: "Well, I think when a man speaks with tongues that his inner being transfers from this area up here (the head) to this area down here (inner being). One of our problems is that we try to think our way through to God by our argumentive minds; but the more we think the more we get involved in ideas and thoughts and theories, when the truth is—God is a Spirit and as Spirit, He must be discerned. Our discerning center is our soul center, and probably it has a lot to do with the innermost being which is sometimes characterized as belly. It is perhaps in this inner being where God moves upon us when our intellect gets in the way. We are supposed to have a particular kind of mind as a follower of Christ, the mind of Christ. 'Let this mind be in you, which was also in Christ Jesus' (Philippians 2:5). We will never have this mind until our mind comes under the control of our spirit and His Spirit. I would say that this is primary."

Reverend Roberts: "Bill, we who have the Holy Spirit remember that even the anticipation of being filled brought joy. The Book of Acts tells us that the 120 returned with joy and waited. There was no hysteria. Jesus had gotten through to them, hadn't He? And when they received on the Day of Pentecost something broke forth, didn't it? They were released. A barrier was broken. They spoke in new tongues, or in tongues new to them. In these new tongues they gave vent to what they felt inside and they magnified God, isn't that right? Now, doesn't Paul say the same thing except with different words? When Paul spoke in tongues it was his spirit speaking to God in prayer or praise, it was his inner being talking to God. And that has to be if we are really to get completely through to God. For example, my mind often tells me everything is OK, but down here the pit of my stomach says, 'No, it's not.' So often the mind tries to feel calm and sure when at the same time there is a terrific churning down deep inside. Since I've been filled with the Spirit and pray in tongues every day, I am helped by the Spirit to find release from such churning. I am edified in my spirit through His Spirit."

Reverend Roberts: "My other question to you, Dr. Reed, is this: What happens to you when you are praying or singing in tongues to God?"

Dr. Reed: "Well, I believe that the primary advantage of praying in tongues is that it gets my argumentative mind out of the picture long enough so that God can operate more fully within me. This is important, because I know that I myself am always going to fall short of the mark. The only hope for me is Christ, the hope of Glory! And He comes into a reality when God Himself anoints my inner being, and I come close to Him in praise and prayer—not just in the words of man's understanding but in the new tongue that the Holy Spirit gives. Doesn't it seem wonderful that God has His own language of the soul which He alone can give us to praise Him with? When we use the language of the soul, which is the language that begins in our spirit by His Spirit and flows upward and out over our tongue, we are really getting release or true edification."

Reverend Roberts: "Bill, look at this fifteenth verse of 1 Corinthians 14: 'I will pray with the Spirit, and I will pray with the understanding also.' Doesn't this mean that Paul prayed first out of his innermost being in tongues and then he followed it with his mind choosing the words and thoughts and prayed in that way?"

Dr. Reed: "Oral, I think something really wonderful is beginning to take place. When we get together in one accord we ought to have more singing in the Spirit. Then we ought to follow that by praying with our intellect and singing with the intellect in our own tongue. This is the way Paul did it."

Reverend Roberts: "Thank you, you have helped us a lot."

Power Release

Now I wish to go a bit further concerning our new tongue.

It is more than an evidence, more than a sign, more than for personal release and edification. *It is also for power release.* When this truth began to dawn on me, I immediately began to examine it; first, by God's Word, next by the experiences of myself and others. When we speak in tongues, power is set in motion and we, as well as others, can be helped enormously by it.

An example of *power release* by a spoken word is seen in the time when I stood up to be married. I was asked to say two words: "I do." When I said, "I do," it was from outward apearances a simple little statement. The truth is that my whole being, and my entire future were involved when I said, "I do." Believe me, I was churning inside and felt a lump in my throat. When I finished saying, "I do," I ended up with a wife. Later four children came along and now I have my first grandchild! Little Brenda Ann Nash. All this because of the two little words, "I do."

In a great storage tank in our city there is an immense amount of water. The problem is to get the water from the tank to us. Usually this is done through a lot of pipes and a little faucet. This little faucet connects with the water and is the instrument through which the water itself is released to us. The little faucet is relatively unimportant, and then again it is very important; because back of that little agent is the water under pressure for release. All you have to do is turn the faucet and instantly the water flows. Now the tongue in itself is relatively unimportant; it is just another member of the physical flesh. It is a physical organ. But when it comes to God it is very important. For the tongue speaks of the total being. When we are speaking in tongues, it is our spirit or our inner being speaking to God.

The very speaking is important. In accepting Christ as our Saviour we do it through believing in our hearts and confessing Christ with our tongues. (Romans 10:9, 10.) There is an inner work and outward manifestation that comes through the use of the tongue. The same is true when one receives the fullness of the Holy Spirit—there is an inner work and the outward manifestation over the tongue. At that instant the tongue is of great value. It is a key. Using my tongue to say, "I do," when nothing is at stake is meaningless. Saying, "I do," at my marriage ceremony is very meaningful. The faucet by itself is nothing. When backed by the pressure of mighty volumes of water, it is tremendously important. When I am filled with the Holy Ghost my tongue is most valuable, because, as I pray in the Spirit, my prayer and my praise to God flow over my tongue in the language of the soul made heavenly by the guidance of the Holy Spirit. In that sense and at that instant, speaking in tongues is *a power release*.

Speaking to God

In 1 Corinthians 14:2, Paul speaks of it as a speaking TO GOD; and in Ephesians 6:18 as "praying in the Spirit" as a part of the whole armor of God in the Christian warfare. In 1 Corinthians Paul says further, ". . . in the Spirit he speaketh mysteries." Take that little term, "in the Spirit." He did not indicate that is the only way to speak to God, but that it is a very vital way to speak to Him. It is speaking IN THE SPIRIT which is the Holy Spirit in reciprocity with the believer's own spirit. (1 Corinthians 14:14, 15.) The Holy Spirit and the believer's spirit act together in harmonious cooperation. It is what is called a divine-human reciprocity. Its aim is to reach God "in the Spirit" rather than only through the mind or intellect. Praying "in the Spirit" is important since, as Paul points out in Ephesians 6:12, "We wrestle not against flesh and blood. . . ." Our warfare is a spiritual one. We can't fight it entirely by our minds. Our minds have definite limitations that the spirit does not have. It is vital that our spirit take precedence over our minds, at certain times, so that our entire inner being can fully respond to God. Paul's advice to the Ephesian believers to add "praying in the Spirit" to their armour must have taken them back to the time when Paul first came to Ephesus and found only about 12 men whom he led into the fullness of the Holy Ghost through the laying on of hands. (Acts 19:1-6.) The Ephesian Church became an explosive force for God through this experience. Not only did they get the new tongue of prayer and praise but prophecy as well. Where tongues is an inspired utterance TO GOD, prophecy is an inspired utterance TO MEN. Both are vital to the witness of the Christian believers.

The Place of Emotion

Every time I pray in tongues, or give thanks to God in tongues, or sing in tongues, I find a point of *power release* in and through me. I feel this. And that feeling is emotion. I heard someone say once that there is no emotion at all involved in speaking with tongues. It is my conviction that such a statement is made defensively, out of a desire to show people that speaking in tongues is not sheer emotionalism. Primarily, speaking in tongues is a spiritual experience. Since it is prayer to God, it is also interpersonal experience. As such it involves the emotions and may cause such emotions as rest, peace, quietness, soft inner glow as well as ecstatic joy which is sometimes, perhaps, overemphasized. So there is an emotional response to the interpersonal relationship with God. But not emotion for emotion's sake, but emotion that is related to truth. For the moment, the intellect relinquishes its absolute control. The believer's spirit in harmony with the Holy Spirit takes over, speaking from the sweetest desire to praise or from the deepest needs of the soul, using the tongue to articulate the words to God. It is emotional, but properly controlled.

The Intellect

At that point the mind is involved to carry out the wishes of the Spirit. For example, I often feel a blossoming of my intellect when I have finished praying or praising God in tongues. Others testify to this same experience. A young man, fresh out of college, testifies that when he heard of the baptism with the Holy Spirit he became hungry. Even though his mind was filled with questions, God acknowledged the hunger of his heart and gave him the fullness of the

Spirit. At that moment, he says, his mind saw issues so clearly that he felt he would never in his whole life think that clearly again. He clung to that moment, even while he was speaking in tongues, to preserve the clarity of illumination. As a result, he says, the Holy Spirit wiped his mind clean and indelibly wrote, "Jesus."

There have been occasions when I have felt such a quickening of my mind following a prayer that I received a "witness" to do some specific thing that resulted in bringing me closer to God. Once I wrote a letter of apology to a friend whom I had previously felt owed me one. Evidently I had developed an "ought against my brother," and had been unable mentally or intellectually to discern what I should do in the matter. While praying with my spirit in the Spirit, the Spirit searched my inner being and found the "ought." From that moment, I had perfect guidance to write a sincere apology. In a few days I received a most gracious apology in return. This was the result of a power release through the Holy Spirit. A divine corrective had been given me. And it was revealed to my mind.

Guidance With Purity

The baptism with the Holy Ghost includes a baptism of fire. (Matthew 3:10.) There is a purity discernible in the life of the Spirit-filled. There is a cleansing of the mind and spirit as one follows the Spirit. Often correctives are given for daily living. The baptism with the Holy Spirit is also to be a "walk in the Spirit." When one is walking, he is going somewhere. Under the guidance of the Spirit, he goes in the right direction which is always toward God and then toward his fellowman to bring God's message of deliverance to him. The walk in the Spirit must be backed by a clean life. One of the Spirit's functions is to help us keep our vessel clean in order that we might be men and women of honest report. (Acts 6:3.)

4 How To Receive the Gift of the Holy Ghost

The Apostle Peter was one of the first Spirit-baptized believers who ever attempted to lead souls to Christ and into receiving the baptism with the Holy Ghost. He preached on the Day of Pentecost under a heavy anointing and his sermon, filled with many prophetic utterances, struck at sin in the hearts of the multitude which had crowded in to "see and hear" what God was doing in the newly "filled" 120 disciples. He showed that the anointed preaching of the gospel is still the most powerful and successful way of bringing conviction for sin to people's hearts. When the crowd cried, "What must we do to be saved?" Peter replied, "Repent, and be baptized every one of you in the name of Jesus Christ for the remission of sins, and ye shall receive the gift of the Holy Ghost" (Acts 2:38).

Think about this a moment. Had you been present that day, this is what you would have been told to do. Peter would have instructed you to receive the baptism with the Holy Ghost with all its enabling power and its new tongue of prayer and praise. He would have told you to move with God into receiving this experience that very hour. You would have felt his urgency and the impelling conviction of God's Spirit in your heart.

Recorded is probably an abbreviated form of Peter's sermon. When he came to the part in which he told them how to receive the gift of the Holy Ghost, he probably took each word and explained it fully. I call to your attention the things which Peter must certainly have stressed in his sermon.

1. Know that the Holy Ghost is a gift to be received, not earned.

A gift is not something that can be earned. If you try to

earn the gift of the Holy Ghost and succeed, then it is a reward and not a gift. I have never been able to accept the idea that anyone can reach a position of merit before God. Once while I was talking about these matters with a husband and wife who were attending one of our seminars at Oral Roberts University, the Holy Spirit began welling up in the wife's innermost being. Words of the Spirit were pressing for utterance, but she would not release them. She would not submit her tongue. When I gently urged her to speak what the Spirit was prompting, she replied, "I can't, I just can't." I asked her why. She said, "Oh, Brother Roberts, I'm just not good enough." I replied, "My sister, unless you change your thinking you will never receive the gift of the Holy Ghost because you nor anyone else can ever be good enough. The Holy Ghost is a gift." She was grateful to receive this information.

2. Put yourself in position to "receive" the gift.

You cannot merit the Holy Ghost but you can "receive" Him as a "gift" from the Father. Knowing this has been a real blessing to me in helping others receive. It does away with straining and begging God. It puts you in a relaxed and receptive mood with childlike dependence upon Jesus to give you what the Father has promised to "give" you.

On the other hand, there are certain conditions you have to meet for receiving this experience. Peter said, "Repent, and be baptized . . . for the remission of sins." Peter says that if you do this YOU SHALL RECEIVE THE GIFT OF THE HOLY GHOST! No *ifs, and's* or *maybe's*. You shall receive. Here we see how vital it is that we repent. This is all-important because we are in the grip of sin until we humble ourselves and turn away from sin so that Christ can master it in our lives. Here also we see that Peter is telling us that if we are to be "filled with the Holy Ghost" we must be "emptied of sin." Only an empty vessel can be filled. Being empty however is still not enough. The empty vessel must be clean or it will contaminate whatever fills it.

If you are to be empty of sin, you must start with repentance. Sin is both an act and a practice that becomes the habit of one's life. The Bible says, "He that committeth sin is of the devil." This habit must be broken, this practice ended, forgiveness received and a new life begun.

Repentance is said to be a change of mind or a turning around. I say it is more than that, and deeper than that. You must admit your sins, facing up to them forthrightly and become sorry for them with Godly sorrow. (2 Corinthians 7:10.) You must reach a place where you are "fed up" with sin, sick and tired of it and through with it. You want the pattern broken up, the practice stopped. You want to live righteously and godly in this present world. You want to be holy before God and man.

Then you must believe that God accepts your repentance and gives you newness of life. It is His life that makes you alive from sins and trespasses. Next, you follow Christ in water baptism. This is very important and essential. It is like the tongue in this regard. It speaks of something from within, an outward testimony that sin is remitted, a new life is begun, a new creature has been born into the Kingdom.

Once you truly repent and experience cleansing from sin, the flow of the river of the Holy Ghost starts. It is here where knowledge of how to receive is indispensible. Think back to the time you really repented and consecrated yourself to God. It was at that point that something started welling up within you. It was the baptism with the Holy Ghost coming, as Jesus described it, "out of your belly" (John 7:38). My experience, and that of many others, is that when sin has been dealt with by God and by you and has been fully cleansed, there is a joy springing up from the innermost being and the Spirit starts giving utterance to speak in a new tongue. Perhaps you have been serving God, and feel that through the cleansing power of Christ's blood sin's pattern has been destroyed in your life. If you will look for it, you will be aware from time to time of this same overflowing joy within you. As that welling up comes again to you, open your mouth and submit your tongue to God.

Lift up your voice but do not attempt to speak in your own language. You cannot speak in two languages at the same time. You may actually hear or see words. Or you may feel something moving in your mouth. We will not all feel the same way, but there will be that surging joy welling up by the Holy Spirit as He seeks to fill us. Remember, your tongue is the expression of your total being. God has designed man so that this little physical instrument in our mouth is the vehicle through which we express everything that we are. We have other ways of expressing ourselves. We can talk to one another without saying a word—by facial expressions, by gestures and motions. But the best way to express ourselves is by the use of the voice. Our whole inner being comes out through the voice. It uses the tongue and the power within becomes a force without.

I could have spoken in tongues a long time before I did had someone instructed me. Too often wrong instructions are given persons preparing to receive the baptism with the Holy Ghost. One should simply be cleansed from sin and enter into the infilling and receiving of the new tongue of power release. Now I know I could have been filled with the Spirit much sooner. I suppose I kept waiting for God to do it all. Many times the Spirit would well up within me, words of another language would enter my mouth, and I stood on the threshold of a new experience. I kept waiting to be overwhelmed, for the new tongue to come pouring forth without my cooperation. It simply wouldn't do it. I suppose we all thought that God did the speaking in tongues, or that the indwelling Christ was the speaker. But why should Jesus speak in tongues since He and His Father are one? He needs no aid to prayer. He reserved that for our limitation.

The Book of Acts (and Paul in 1 Corinthians 14) show that it is by the Spirit's prompting and by our using the vocal organs that we speak with tongues. "And THEY spoke with tongues, as the SPIRIT gave them utterance" (Acts 2:4).

I felt this many times before I had the boldness to speak forth by faith what I felt welling up within me. At last I became willing to speak some of the strange words forming in my mouth. Only a few, maybe four or five at first, formed. When I spoke them, that was the beginning of something new and promising for my Christian witness. I received an instant release in my spirit and was tremendously edified. It was later that I began to understand that the purpose of my new language was to speak to God *with my spirit in THE SPIRIT*, and that it was a source of power release. I continued speaking in tongues through the years and each time with profound depths of edification.

It was in 1961 that God began to deal with me directly about speaking in the Spirit more frequently and with more understanding. He led me into a careful study of His Word again concerning the Holy Ghost and the value of tongues. Gradually I was given more light on the subject and found myself hungering for more of this experience. One of the first things that happened was a determination to find the frequency of Paul who thanked God that, "I speak with tongues MORE THAN YE ALL." Ephesians 6:18 inspired me to believe that as often as I prayed, which has always been very frequently, I should and could use my new tongue devotionally toward God. I too thank God for the richness and depth and dimension of this experience which is daily in my life. Christ who has been my very life over the years seems to have become even more real. It seems I love Him so much that sometimes my heart feels it will burst. There is more power in my ministry, more self-control, more eagerness and release. This is what makes it valid and valuable to me. Anything that brings me more of Christ is my interest.

One thing is certain. Jesus Himself is the baptizer. "He shall baptize you with the Holy Ghost . . . and with fire" (Matthew 3:11). We are not taught by the Word of God to seek a thing. We are taught to seek a Person, the Lord Jesus Christ. When we ask Him for the gift of the Holy Ghost, He will give it to us. You can approach Christ with all confidence, knowing that you will receive exactly what you ask, and that what you receive will be exactly what He wants you to have.

It is my conviction that the welling up within always

follows the work of God's grace that remits sin. This peace and joy that wells up within us originates with God. It is there a great deal of the time. You need to become aware of this, expect it and cooperate with it. Perhaps you sense it in a different way or call it by a different name. *Some experience a stirring within, a quickening presence, or a warm awareness or a coming upon.* It is sometimes described as an awareness of God's infilling presence. I have yet to ask a Christian if he ever feels this presence welling up within him who didn't say, "Yes, many times." Usually he adds, "But I did not know what it was."

In receiving the baptism with the Holy Ghost you need to take yourself out of the realm of fear. And resistance to receiving must be overcome. You need to study God's Word and know that His highest desire is for you to be filled with the Spirit and to walk in the Spirit. You need to consider that Jesus Himself is the baptizer, and that what He gives you is good. Also, you need to know the value of yielding your whole being to Christ, submitting your entire self to Him with joy and thanksgiving.

The disciples were lifted from the depths of despair through listening to Jesus tell them about the baptism with the Holy Ghost. As they began to comprehend the power they would receive and the new tongue of prayer and praise they would be given, they became willing for Jesus to leave, physically. The joy of expectation took despair and fear away, infusing them with desire to receive the Holy Ghost.

Doubtless many things Jesus had told them about receiving the Holy Spirit came to their minds at this time; especially, Luke 11:9-13.

"And I say unto you, Ask, and it shall be given you; seek, and ye shall find; knock, and it shall be opened unto you. For every one that asketh receiveth; and he that seeketh findeth; and to him that knocketh it shall be opened. If a son shall ask bread of any of you that is a father, will he give him a stone? or if he asks a fish, will he for a fish give him a serpent? or if he shall ask an egg, will he offer him a scorpion? If ye then, being evil, know how to give good gifts unto your children: how much more shall your heavenly Father give the Holy Spirit to them that ask him?"

Jesus teaches us to *ask* for the Holy Spirit. Simply ask. We have discovered the value of telling our friends to ask only *once*. There is no place for begging or pleading for the Holy Spirit when the Lord is more eager for you to be filled than you are. Ask sincerely and ask believingly that He will give you the Holy Spirit.

Next, your *will* is involved. Your intellect is partially bypassed for the moments you will be speaking in tongues. That is because it is your spirit praying rather than your mind forming the thought and speech patterns. On the other hand, God gave you your intellect and works through it constantly. It takes an act of your will to ask God for the Holy Spirit, and an act of your will in cooperation with the Holy Spirit to speak in a new tongue. There comes a time in receiving the Holy Spirit when you have to bend your intellect and submit your tongue to Christ, because your tongue speaks from out of your total being. Only as you surrender your tongue are you surrendering everything. It's the nature of the case.

As a child of God you often engage in prayer. How do you do this? Isn't it by an act of your *will* as well as an act of your faith? It isn't easy always to pray or to give thanks to God. We have to will or determine to do it, don't we? In the same way when the Spirit wells up within you, that is the signal for you to respond, to surrender to God your intellect and your tongue and speak forth in the new tongue of prayer and praise. Your spirit desires to break through intellectual barriers and limitations and speak to God free and unfettered. The soul is seeking to be edified by your speaking "in the Spirit."

Recently we were praying with a Harvard University graduate who was hungry to receive the Holy Ghost. His great mind got in the way at first but as we continued talking about the need of his spirit to pray, and that praying in the Spirit was perhaps Paul's favorite way of praying, he became deeply interested and eager to have this experience. One day while asking Christ to give him this gift, five or six words came to him which he spoke forth in rather halting fashion. He said to me, "Oral, I thought there would be a volume of words and that they would rush out of my mouth." I replied, "This rarely happens since most of us do not talk in our own tongue in that way. Our normal way of speaking is in a quiet controlled voice." I think he was looking for something that was more or less abnormal to him. I reminded him that my first words in tongues were also few but that I persevered in the Spirit until I spoke in tongues almost in volumes. He said, "That's what I want." I replied, "This, you can have. But first accept what God has begun to give you." He said, "How do I know this is from God?" I asked, "When you speak those few words to God, what do you feel in your inner being?" His face lighted up, he smiled and said, "Glorious, just glorious." I said, "Then it is from God. Whatever is good is from God." Then I recalled Jesus' words: "If a son shall ask bread of any of you that is a father, will he give him a stone? . . . How much more shall your heavenly Father give the Holy Spirit to them that ask him?" I said, "You asked God for the gift of the Holy Ghost, didn't you?" He said, "Yes." I said, "What did He give you?" He said, "Well, He gave me these few words and this glorious feeling within when I spoke them." I said, "In other words, you asked for bread and God gave you bread. You asked for the Holy Ghost and God gave you the Holy Ghost." He said, "What am I to do now?" I said, "Use your new tongue every day to pray in the Holy Spirit and to give thanks with your spirit. Gradually you will become more fluent in the Spirit. You will ultimately go from language to language and find edification and a closeness to God you can have in no other way." He said, "That's what I desire more than anything else in the world."

It has happened to him since, exactly as we knew it would.

One woman after receiving the Holy Spirit and speaking in tongues burst into tears, saying, "Oh, I could have had this eight years ago. I know the joy I am experiencing now tried to enter me then."

Do not wait for the Holy Ghost to do it all. You must respond with your faith. Allow the Holy Spirit to speak through you. Cooperate with Him. As you do, you will have all at once a new awareness and a new intimacy with God. You will be released. You will experience a liberation and expansion in your spirit. When you have finished speaking the first words under the inspiration of the Spirit your mind will blossom. Things hidden in your spirit which the mind could not find will be brought out before you. The Holy Spirit knows exactly what is needed and how to bring it out. You will be given divine correctives for your life. Your desire to make wrongs right will be sharpened. Jesus will become more real to you. God's Word will take on a new dimension. You will want to read it as though you had never read it before. Your discernment will be increased; speaking with tongues will become a point of *power release*.

Many sincere believers ask, "Do I have to speak with tongues? If so, why?" It isn't as much a matter of feeling you have to, as it is understanding that God has given you this privilege. As you know, you speak from your inner being through your tongue. Paul said in 1 Corinthians 14:14, "For if I pray in an unknown tongue, my spirit prayeth. . . ." In other words: my inner being prayeth, my inner being speaks and my tongue is the vehicle.

I have stated, when Evelyn and I stood up to be married, I simply said two words, "I do." When I said those two words twenty-five years ago, I gave my being to my wife. I said the words with my tongue, but they came out of my inner being. My total self was speaking. My tongue was the vehicle. That's how it is when we speak with tongues. Paul says our spirit is speaking . . . that is, speaking to God. (1 Corinthians 14:2.)

If the *full* force of the Holy Ghost is to be released, it will have to come over our tongue, because our tongue is the expression of our total inner self. And this is why we may speak in tongues daily, because the Holy Ghost is within.

It is by our desire and by the desire of the Holy Spirit, by the exercise of our will and the exercise of the will of the Holy Spirit, through an act of faith, that we may speak at any moment. The whole experience is based on faith. It is a cooperative act, a divine-human reciprocity. Reciprocity is actually two forces acting on each other. For example, behind the faucet the water is pushing to get release. The faucet lets the water come forth. They join and there comes a flood of water. So likewise, here is the Holy Spirit welling up within us and here is our tongue. The two cooperate and there comes a flood of inner self-expression and spiritual edification. *Without the Holy Spirit I cannot, but without me He will not.*

3. Be willing to bypass your intellect.

Our intellect is one of the great forces that makes us different from all other creatures. We are thankful for our intellect. This is the age of reason. Our intellect is that against which we struggle the longest. We do not want to submit it. But God is Spirit and He cannot be reasoned out. Years ago I was almost beside myself trying to reason this out. Paul reached a point where he had to bend his intellect, and if he could bend his giant intellect we can certainly afford to bend ours. At times he had to quit talking in his own language and quit thinking in his own mind. He simply prayed in tongues and let his spirit reach upward to God. As this was valid and valuable for Paul, it is a precious privilege for us also.

When we pray we sometimes reach a place in our minds where we cannot express what is in our spirits, what is in our total inner man. We have to bypass our mind and make it inactive for the moment. The mind slips into the background during the moments we are praying in tongues and remains in a state of neutrality. But down in our inner man our spirit is really talking to God and using the tongue for its total expression. We are either telling Him what is in our hearts through prayer, through thanks and praise or through singing. And when we do that, we are edified. Our spirit is released.

4. The Holy Spirit will flow forth as a river.

Jesus described this experience as a river flowing from within us. A river starts small but grows larger and wider and stronger until it becomes irresistible. Finally it ends in the ocean. Usually when we first speak in tongues we do not say many words, though some people do. My experience did not begin with a large vocabulary. But I tell you the truth, it was like electricity within me. Something happened in my inner being. I felt as though I could have flown away. I felt the love of God, and immediately I said, "Lord, let me speak again!" He did let me speak again and for several moments I just talked in tongues, then stopped and rejoiced for a while in my own language and then spoke more in other tongues. From that time on I desired to speak every day in tongues, but strangely enough, I was not able to do so for several months. But I was determined that God would give me this release every day.

Finally He gave me release. Every morning when I waken, the Holy Spirit and I begin the day by praying in tongues. My entire being is opened up and there is a blossoming of my intellect. Then I follow by choosing in my own mind my own words. Tongues are not a little tributary of the river, but they are the mainstream of a mighty flowing river. And I can truthfully say that I have a continual love feast with the Lord by praying in the Spirit.

The baptism with the Holy Spirit is a tremendous experience. It is the descent of God in greater fullness into man and the ascent of man more completely into God. It is God and total man blended in oneness. It is really a miracle. Would you like to have that inner release of your spirit? When you experience that release you will have no questions about whether or not you are baptized with the Holy Ghost. From that day forward you will begin a new spiritual encounter with the Holy Spirit your Comforter and the Lord Jesus Christ your Saviour. He can give you a supernatural utterance daily, because He abides with you forever. The experience will be an edification and a therapy in your spiritual life. You can accept it today. Do not sit on the sidelines and just be a spectator in this great move of the Holy Ghost today. Why don't you ask Him right now!!!

5   Stirring Up the Gift Within

After being filled with the Spirit, you are to "walk in the Spirit." Walking in the Spirit means that you are going somewhere. You are on a mission for your Saviour, the Lord Jesus Christ. You are His own witness. He is the joy of your heart. Sharing Him with others is the greatest privilege of all. What opportunities you have every day!

Remember that the Holy Spirit is not in your heart as a guest who spoke when He entered and never will speak again. The Spirit wants to enter into a harmonious cooperation with you so that you may pray in the Spirit often. Paul counseled his beloved Ephesian brethren to be "PRAYING ALWAYS IN THE SPIRIT" (Ephesians 6:18).

Through the years, I have found that praying in tongues is of value to me both in my devotions and in the ministry of praying for the sick. It is also helpful when the sick can pray in the Spirit. People are not only sick with diseases, they are sick in other ways too. People are prone to live with all kinds of negatives bottled up inside them. Eventually the person himself becomes ill. Jesus gave power to heal sickness and disease. (Matthew 10:1.) He did not stop there, however, He knew that was not enough. He gave the charge to "heal the sick" (Matthew 10:8). He implemented this by saying "And heal the sick that are therein, and say unto them, The kingdom of God is come nigh unto you" (Luke 10:9). Jesus wants the whole man healed. This is illustrated in the responses of the ten lepers after Jesus cleansed their bodies of leprosy. One returned to Jesus to give thanks. Jesus said, "Were there not ten cleansed? Where are the nine?" He indicated that although ten were healed of leprosy only one became a "whole man."

PUTTING KINDLING ON THE FIRE

Before I enter a healing line I often pray quietly in tongues until I am edified and released. As I pray in the Spirit I feel love coming out of my heart, accompanied with a greater vitality in my body. Praying for the sick uses up a great deal of my physical strength. I find that praying in the Spirit seems to help restore vitality. This is one reason I feel that Paul was referring to praying in tongues when he told Timothy: "Wherefore I put thee in remembrance that thou stir up the gift of God, which is in thee by the putting on of my hands" (2 Timothy 1:6).

In this remarkable passage there appears to be a definite reference to the bestowal of the gift of the Holy Ghost through the laying on of Paul's hands. This entire passage is as follows: "I thank God, whom I serve from my forefathers with pure conscience, that without ceasing I have remembrance of thee in my prayers night and day; Greatly desiring to see thee, being mindful of thy tears, that I may be filled with joy; When I call to remembrance the unfeigned faith that is in thee, which dwelt first in thy grandmother Lois, and thy mother Eunice; and I am persuaded that in thee also. Wherefore I put thee in remembrance that thou stir up the gift of God, which is in thee by the putting on of my hands" (2 Timothy 1:3-6). This passage is commonly interpreted as referring to Timothy's ordination. But his ordination to the ministry is referred to in Paul's first letter which reads, "Neglect not the gift that is in thee, which was given thee by prophecy, with the laying on of the hands of the presbytery" (1 Timothy 4:14). Not only is the phrasing of the two passages very different, the contexts are entirely different. It may well be the case that in 2 Timothy 1:6, Paul is referring, not to Timothy's ordination, but to his being baptized with the Holy Ghost. If this is true, and the evidence supports it, this would bring it into harmony with Acts 19:1-6 where it is strongly implied

that part of Paul's normal procedure was to lay on hands
so that believers would receive the gift of the Holy Ghost.
If this application is correct, 2 Timothy 1:6 is of decisive
importance, and gives clear proof that Paul was urging
Timothy to stir up the gift of the Holy Ghost in him by
speaking in tongues more often; and thereby, as stated in
verses 7 and 8, overcoming fear by releasing the spirit of
power and love and self-control. This interpretation is further
reinforced by the contrast between the spirit of fear (including timidity in its worst form) and the spirit of power,
of *agape*, and of self-control. These gifts are the normal gifts
of the Holy Spirit (1 Corinthians 12:7-11) to Spirit-filled
believers, and not gifts specially linked with the ordination
of a man to the ministry.

Paul's language to Timothy suggests that we engage in this
spiritual exercise frequently for power release. He reminded
him to "Stir up the gift of God, which is in thee by the
putting on of my hands, FOR God hath not given us the
spirit of fear; but of POWER, and of LOVE, and of a
SOUND MIND." These things—power, love, self-control—are
stimulated in me when the Holy Spirit like a river flows
through me frequently. It helps me overcome fear. While
praying in the Spirit, I face fear in the realm where it has
its existence, the realm of the spirit. My mind helps, but
much of the time my mind is not entirely able to eject fear
nor to keep it from entering. Praying in the Spirit, I feel
power rising up from within, I feel love, God's love. Sometimes I feel it like a river flowing. It is then that I have
the greatest self-control.

I cannot begin to emphasize the importance of having self-
control particularly while praying for the sick. In the healing
line, I face virtually every kind of demon; virtually all types
of sickness and disease; as well as fear, despair, doubt and even
unbelief. At the same time, I am confronted with my own
human weaknesses and inabilities. At such a time, praying
in the Spirit does not provide all the answers nor is it a cure
all. But I can honestly say that it really helps.

Let us see what happens when you pray in the Spirit or

when you speak in tongues. Paul tells us, "He that speaketh in an unknown tongue edifieth himself" (1 Corinthians 14:4). Self-edification is important to the spiritual health and well-being of every Christian. Jude exhorts us: "Beloved, building up yourselves on your most holy faith, praying in the Holy Ghost" (verse 20). The Holy Spirit knows how and when we need edification, for the Spirit searches the heart:

"The Spirit also helpeth our infirmities: for we know not what we should pray for as we ought: but the Spirit itself [Himself] maketh intercession for us with groanings which cannot be uttered.

"And he that searcheth the hearts knoweth what is the mind of the Spirit, because he maketh intercession for the saints according to the will of God" (Rom. 8:26, 27).

What is meant by "the Spirit itself [Himself] maketh intercession for us with groanings which cannot be uttered"? There are blessed times when we are able to get through to God in earnest prayer in our own language. However, at other times we are mute before our burden. The emotions we feel or the burdens we want to talk with God about are so great that we sigh inwardly, finding no words that can adequately express the depth of what we feel and long for. At such times, the Holy Spirit searches out and prays from deep within our heart and soul, giving utterances to the deepest longings and needs of our soul in a way that we cannot, with words that flow from our spirit over our tongue. We are no longer hampered by shyness or inhibitions. We are not overly concerned about word-phrasing. We are submerged in the flooding tide of the rivers of living water that are surging up within us as our self-consciousness and inhibitions are released.

This is one of the most exquisite experiences the soul has on earth. The Person of the Holy Spirit takes control of our inner self, the self that only the Spirit fully knows, and prays directly to God, expressing to Him our deepest desires.

When we pray in tongues, it is the Spirit that speaks. It is a direct, intimate, straight-to-God communication. Our prayer is getting through to the Heavenly Father, because the

Spirit prays "according to the will of God" for us. He takes our shapeless prayers and gives them form. It is the prayer of the Spirit Himself—our prayer joined with His prayer on our behalf, rather than our prayer alone.

A DIVINE THERAPIST

I am told that, among other things, a psychiatrist is a professionally trained listener who knows how to question you so that you can talk about the things hidden and repressed in your spirit that are troubling you. The psychiatrist searches and finds ways to help you bring them out into the open and talk them out. Then you feel released. The Holy Spirit is a divine Therapist. He gets down inside your inner being and finds these things that are troubling you. As you speak in the language of the Spirit, the therapy is going on and that is why you feel instantly relieved or edified.

This does not mean that speaking in tongues is a "cure-all." It does mean that God responds and places divine aids at your disposal: knowledge, divine insight, prophecy or some doctrine or teaching on the matter. (1 Corinthians 14:6.) Through them God gives you help to solve the problem. You are relieved; therefore, the problem becomes different, because you look at it differently.

This is one of the most meaningful lessons I have ever learned. The divine therapy of the Holy Spirit is exactly what took place in my life when I was given a divine corrective to write the letter of apology to which I have already referred. He searched out my inner being and performed divine therapy in my soul. I did not confer with a human being. I felt an urge to speak in tongues to Him, and when I did the Spirit was able to redirect me into a right course of action toward a brother in Christ.

Paul spoke of two ways to pray. He said, "I will pray with the spirit, and I will pray with the understanding also" (1 Corinthians 14:15). The human spirit is subject to our human will. Paul said, "The spirits of the prophets are subject to the prophets" (verse 32). Therefore, when we speak with tongues, we willingly yield to the Holy Spirit. And our *willing* cooperativeness with the Spirit who gives utterance produces both prayer and praise.

It seems that often, after Paul had prayed in the Spirit, he followed that prayer with prayer with his intellect and in his own language. Both ways are scriptural. Both are vital to our spiritual health.

YOUR WILL IS INVOLVED

The *will* is involved in both types of praying, but in a different way. If you will to pray with the intellect, you make use of a prerogative which God has granted to the *will*. You *will* to focus the mind on the particular thoughts, and you *will* to speak or think the words which express them. If you *will* to pray in the Spirit, you are exercising a prerogative to respond to what the Spirit desires to say through you. You may *will* to refuse to respond to the prompting of the Spirit, and thus quench the Spirit. In situations where human exuberance tempts you to utterances in the flesh when the Spirit is not prompting a manifestation in tongues you may *will* to subdue the flesh and wait for a genuine leading of the Spirit. In instances where your judgment tells you that prayer aloud in the Spirit would be out of order you may *will* to pray quietly within yourself and to God.

In the same way, Paul sang or praised God. "I will sing with the spirit," he said, "and I will sing with the understanding also" (1 Corinthians 14:15).

Singing in tongues does not necessarily mean singing a song that is set to music. The singing in Paul's day was usually a psalm through which they expressed either praise or supplication, or both. Paul indicates that he praised God in tongues first, then he praised God in his own tongue.

By yielding his spirit and tongue to the Holy Spirit, he was able to express the heights and depths of what his soul felt. This gave him release and freedom within. He was built up in spirit and strengthened and better prepared to prophesy or do other things for God.

No wonder Paul said, "I thank my God, I speak with tongues more than ye all" (1 Corinthians 14:18). Only the exquisite joy of speaking in tongues could have caused him to make such a statement. This frequent experience became such a great spiritual power in Paul's life that he thanked God for the privilege of speaking and praying with tongues more frequently than the entire Corinthian Church to which his letter was directed.

It is a meaningful privilege to pray with our spirit IN THE SPIRIT as often as we have need.

6 The Major Purpose of the Gift of Tongues

The Apostle Paul speaks of a gift of divers kinds of tongues, and a gift of interpretation of tongues. (1 Corinthians 12:10.) Speaking in tongues in the gift form does not have the same purpose as what I call "simple tongues." The simple tongues of prayer and praise are for personal edification and release in your own spirit after you have received the infilling of the Holy Spirit. In its gift form, speaking in tongues has a larger purpose altogether. The one speaking in tongues through the (manifestation of the) gift of divers kinds of tongues goes beyond edifying himself. He exercises the gift of tongues when he is with a body of believers either in a church meeting or a smaller group. (1 Corinthians 14:26-28.) In the group there is a larger and more diverse need of edification. This need can be met through a combination of the last two of the nine gifts of the Spirit, the gift of divers kinds of tongues and the gift of interpretation of tongues.

When one is filled with the Holy Spirit and continues to walk in the Spirit, he is given a special ability to pray or praise God in tongues. Through it he edifies himself, a need which he has often. (1 Corinthians 14:4, 18.) In the gift form, tongues have special power to edify and release *other* believers to edify the body of Christ. Both are valuable experiences to strengthen and build up believers. (Jude 20.)

The following references to tongues in the fourteenth chapter of First Corinthians appear to be related in a special way: "He that SPEAKETH IN AN UNKNOWN TONGUE *speaketh not unto men, but unto God*: for no man understandeth him; howbeit in the spirit he speaketh mysteries" (verse 2). "He that SPEAKETH IN AN UNKNOWN TONGUE *edifieth himself*" (4). "I would that *ye all* SPAKE WITH TONGUES" (5). "Wherefore let him that SPEAKETH IN AN UNKNOWN TONGUE *pray that he may interpret.* For if I pray in an unknown tongue, my spirit prayeth, but my understanding is unfruitful. What is it then? *I will pray* WITH THE SPIRIT, and I will pray with the understanding also: *I will sing* WITH THE SPIRIT, and I will sing with the understanding also. Else when thou shalt *bless* WITH THE SPIRIT, how shall he that occupieth the room of the unlearned say Amen at thy *giving of thanks,* seeing he understandeth not what thou sayest? For thou verily givest thanks well, but the other is not edified. I thank my God, I SPEAK WITH TONGUES more than ye all: yet in the church I had rather speak five words with my understanding, that by my voice I might teach others also, than ten thousand words IN AN UNKNOWN TONGUE" (13-19). ". . . *forbid not* to SPEAK WITH TONGUES" (39). In these references Paul seems to be referring to simple devotional tongues which he wishes that all spake.

Another series of references in the twelfth chapter of the first Corinthian letter also appears to be related in a special way. "To one is given by the Spirit the word of wisdom . . . to another DIVERS KINDS OF TONGUES; to another the INTERPRETATION OF TONGUES" (verses 8, 10). "Do all SPEAK WITH TONGUES? do all INTERPRET?" (30). "There are differences of administrations, but the same Lord. And there are diversities of operation, but it is the same God which worketh all in all" (5, 6). "For as *the body is one, and hath many members,* and all the members of that one body, being many, are one body: so also is Christ" (12). "And if they were all one member, where were the body?" (19). "Now *ye are the body* of Christ, *and members in particular.* And God hath set some in the church, first apostles, secondarily prophets, thirdly teachers, after that miracles, then gifts of healings, helps, governments, DIVERSITIES OF TONGUES" (27, 28). Paul here seems to refer to the gift of tongues and its companion, the gift of interpretation of tongues, and to the order and procedure in which they are to be exercised.

In simple tongues, the Spirit-filled believer speaks to God

and finds real help in this divine expression; he needs no one with him, it can be a personal experience only. In the gift of tongues, the believer speaks to God in behalf of the needs of others. Speaking in tongues, like any other manifestation of the Spirit, is given to meet needs. Everyone has needs, both spiritual and physical. "Likewise the Spirit . . . helpeth our infirmities [needs]" (Romans 8:26).

NEED OF THE GIFT OF TONGUES

How does the gift of tongues work today to meet the needs of people?

1. There is the need in a group of believers for edification. Edification means to be strengthened and built up in the inner man. Jude refers to this: "Building up yourselves on your most holy faith, praying in the Holy Ghost" (Jude 20).

Notice the very important position of one in the Church who exercises both the gift of tongues and interpretation of tongues. (This person is fully equal to the one exercising the gift of prophecy.) "I would that ye all spake with tongues, but rather that ye prophesied: for greater is he that prophesieth than he that speaketh with tongues, except he interpret, that the church may receive edifying. Now, brethren, if I come unto you speaking with tongues, what shall I profit you, except I shall speak to you either by revelation, or by knowledge, or by prophesying, or by doctrine?" (1 Corinthians 14:5, 6).

It is sometimes said that tongues plus interpretation equals prophecy. Paul does not say that. What he says is that a speaker in tongues plus an interpretation is equal to a speaker of prophecy. This is a truth that Paul wishes us to see. If tongues, plus interpretation, equals prophecy, why did God set the gift of tongues and interpretation in the Church at all? Why not seven gifts instead of nine? The gift of tongues and interpretation of tongues may have a form of prophecy as one of its functions, as we will see later, but prophecy has a much larger function than in the form it is manifested through tongues and interpretation.

Here I want to comment on Paul's statement in 1 Corinthians 12:31: "Covet the best gifts." Does he mean some gifts are better than others and are to be desired more? In 1 Corinthians 14:1 he says, "Desire spiritual gifts." Who can say which is the best gift? Who can say which one of His gifts is the best? Is it not the gift needed at the time? If the need were for spiritual insight and perception, would not the gift of the word of knowledge be the best gift? If the need were for healing, would not a gift of healing be best? If the need were for edification, would not the gift of tongues and interpretation be best?

2. Interpretation of divers kinds of tongues provides the edification needed. Through the gift of tongues, one speaks to God within a wider scope and larger purpose than he does through simple tongues. He goes beyond edifying himself to edifying the entire group. As he begins to speak in tongues in its gift form, the Spirit senses the needs of the believers, gathers up these needs and prays through the tongue of the believer to God. Paul states what is actually happening during this prayer. "Likewise the Spirit also helpeth our infirmities: for we know not what we should pray for as we ought: but the Spirit itself maketh intercession for us with groanings which cannot be uttered. And he that searcheth the hearts knoweth what is the mind of the Spirit, because he maketh intercession for the saints according to the will of God" (Romans 8:26, 27). The Spirit is praying through the one with the gift of tongues making intercession *"for the saints according to the will of God."* At this moment, the Spirit is "searching the hearts," and gathering up the longings and desires and expressing them, through divers kinds of tongues, to God. The Spirit is searching out the inhibitions, hidden resentments, repressions and scars that are imbedded in the human spirit and sending them up to God. The Spirit knows how to pray and for what to pray that Christ may be complete in us. *The Spirit prays in the will of God and in the mind of the Spirit in behalf of those present.* He not only knows their hearts and their needs, but he knows exactly what God's will is regarding each of these needs. He gives

utterance through the believer in tongues with groanings which cannot be uttered or for which there is no equivalent expression in human thought. Those groanings can only be expressed in "divers kinds of tongues," tongues that are unknown to the understanding. Being incapable for the moment of formulating words or phrases with which accurately and fully to unburden ourselves, we rely on the Holy Spirit who knows how to intercede.

Beneath the outer layer of our being, there is the inner self or the real self. This is what the Spirit searches through simple tongues when the Spirit-filled believer prays in the Spirit. Likewise, this is what the gift of tongues searches—for the purpose of releasing the ones present and edifying their inner being.

How does one know when simple tongues which he uses in his own devotions merge with the gift of divers kinds of tongues through which he ministers in behalf of others? I have found through my own experience and through that of many others that when the gift of tongues begins to operate the believer finds himself moved and inspired in a different kind of way. He becomes acutely aware of the needs of those who are present and God's great desire to meet them. At that time when he speaks in tongues, it is not only in his own behalf but in behalf of others. His voice seems to take on a different tone and resonance—not louder but a normal speaking tone. He may remain seated quietly or stand in an unobtrusive manner. In his normal speaking voice, he begins to speak in tongues, speaking to God in a more intense way, with a deeper compassion and ordinarily in a larger volume of words. What is happening? The Spirit is manifesting the gift of tongues in behalf of the body of Christ where there is a need for edification that can be met only in this way.

Paul makes it clear that not every believer can manifest a gift of tongues. While every Spirit-filled believer may speak in (simple) tongues to edify himself, he can only manifest the gift of tongues if the Spirit wills for him to do so. Paul asked these questions in 1 Corinthians 12:29, 30: "Are all apostles? are all prophets? are all teachers? are all workers of miracles? Have all the gifts of healing? do all speak with tongues? do all interpret?" Here he points out that the Spirit manifests different gifts in different believers. This includes the gift of tongues and interpretation of tongues. *Only the Holy Spirit can determine when to manifest any of the nine gifts through a believer to meet the needs that are present.* A believer may feel a degree of some particular gift present in him at any given moment which he may exercise in his own behalf or in an ordinary way for others. This is the simple form of it. When the full gift is manifested, however, there is an immediate heightening of the Spirit's power through the believer; his compassion toward others is aroused, and his attention is focused on their needs and God's delivering power.

Very frequently in my ministry a gift of healing will be manifested in me. A much higher percentage of people is healed when this gift is present. At other times, healing is manifested through me in its simple form. I know when the gift is present and when it is not. The people who are present usually know when the gift is there too. One can do so much more to meet the needs of people when the gifts of the Spirit are being manifested through him.

My experience with the gift of tongues, as with other gifts of the Spirit, is that when it is present, the power of God is manifested in a more pronounced way. *The believer exercising a gift of tongues is really possessed of God at that time.* The gift and the believer seem to become one. Together, the believer and the gift become God's instrument to meet certain needs of the people.

It seems that in Paul's day, the services of the church were more informal than today. The pomp, ceremony and ritual that we know today had not come into vogue. The emphasis seemed to be upon manifestations of the Holy Spirit more, and less upon the human part. For example, Paul urged in each meeting, "When you come together, [let] every one of you hath a psalm, hath a doctrine, hath a tongue, hath a revelation, hath an interpretation. Let all things be done unto edifying" (1 Corinthians 14:26).

This was actually his suggested pattern of worship when the believers met together in a group meeting that was not necessarily a large public meeting. One was to give one of the psalms of God, another to bring forth a doctrine of God's Word, another was to exercise a gift of healing, another a gift of tongues and interpretation, another a revelation or word of knowledge. Each of these things was to be done in a way to edify and strengthen those present.

It is our experience that when a gift of tongues is being exercised, a holy hush falls over the group. Instantly the people enter into the mood of the Spirit as a manifestation of tongues is interceding in their behalf. Then the group waits for the gift of interpretation to interpret *God's response and confirmation* of what is in the mind of the Spirit for them. This is ordinarily called *a message in tongues. It is more correctly a manifestation of tongues and interpretation.* Interpretation is the key that unlocks the mysteries to which expression is given through tongues. "Howbeit in the Spirit, he speaketh mysteries" (1 Corinthians 14:2). This refers to "secret truths" which require interpretation to be understood.

The believer exercising the gift of divers kinds of tongues may proceed from one form of utterance to another—that is, from tongue to tongue. A variety in the tongues spoken may be directed to a diversity in the needs present. In this case the speaker may speak in divers kinds of tongues before there is any interpretation. Then, when the needs have been spoken to God, the gift of interpretation will be manifested.

7 Suggestions for Exercising a Gift of Tongues

Speaking in tongues in your devotions is for your own edification. Usually only you are involved and much of the time you do it when you are alone. In manifesting a GIFT OF TONGUES, you go beyond edifying yourself and become a ministering servant of God. The Holy Spirit manifests this gift of the Spirit through you in behalf of the needs of others. For this reason you are acting in a position of responsibility. While you may not be an ordained minister of the gospel, a great many of the same rules that are applicable to him apply to you. These include personal responsibility for the use of your gift before God and man. You are affecting lives other than your own. You affect them in a very personal and direct way. Through the gift of tongues manifested through you, the Holy Spirit is endeavoring "to intercede and plead before God in behalf of the saints according to and in harmony with God's will" (Romans 8:27, Amplified).

This is no little thing. You become God's instrument. A gift is manifested through you. With this privilege comes:

1. Personal responsibility.

You become responsible for the use of the gift. The use of the gift of tongues is included in Paul's admonition: "Let all things be done unto edifying" (1 Corinthians 14:26). The Amplified Version gives it: "Let everything be constructive and edifying and for the good of all." *You are responsible to edify those present.* If you exercise a gift in a manner that is for the good of all present, you are a responsible and effective witness of Jesus Christ; if not, you are a poor witness.

You are also responsible to understand the function of your gift and to know how and when to exercise it.

Not only is speech through the Holy Ghost power; knowledge is power. The ultimate purpose of every gift of the Spirit is to reveal Jesus Christ, to testify of Him and to enable believers to be more complete in Him. While it takes faith to exercise a gift of the Spirit, it takes knowledge and wisdom to do it in the most effective way.

Many who feel the Spirit would manifest a gift of tongues through them are little more than babes in Christ. Yet we can take encouragement even in this for God can reveal knowledge to babes. (Luke 10:21.) An old woodsman was once asked why his ax seemed to cut better than those of his fellows. "I keep it sharp, Sir," he replied, "I find a sharp ax cuts better than a dull one." This is another way of saying that knowledge and wisdom go hand in hand with applied power.

You are to manifest your gift in an orderly fashion. "If any man speak in an unknown tongue, let it be by two, or at the most by three, and that by course; and let one interpret. But if there be no interpreter, let him keep silence in the church; and let him speak to himself, and to God" (1 Corinthians 14:27, 28). You are to take your turn, not monopolize time that is to be shared with others. The ability to exercise a gift of tongues is not to be displayed as a badge of honor. Rather, the very presence of such a gift reflects the goodness of God and His desire to edify believers. One should be a part of God's over-all program. Feeling superior has no place among God's people. No one is divinely perfect and no one has all God has. At his very best, he still falls short. He must act responsibly and conduct himself humbly and in love.

In a sense, you and a gift are one with the Spirit. You can act in a way that causes the gift to shine with the glory of God and to reflect what God is and what He wants to do. Your motivation for exercising the gift is *ágape* or divine love.

You are responsible to be in control of your spirit. "And the spirits of the prophets [the speakers in tongues] are subject to the prophets" (1 Corinthians 14:32). This is self-control. We are all emotional beings but we are not to respond or react purely on emotion. To have emotion is a fine thing. (Emotion is part of a normal response to truth.) Emotion for emotion's sake is sheer emotionalism and has no justification in exercising a gift of the Spirit or of responding to it. The Spirit may bypass your understanding in order to produce the utterance in tongues, but at the same time it is functioning in you to help you to exercise good judgment and function through your understanding.

Referring to the proper and improper use of emotion in speaking with tongues, the Rev. Dennis Bennett gave this illustration: "We don't think it strange when the crowd cheers a touchdown or even works up a few cheers when the team is having a rough time. We would if they cheered when the team is not on the field."

A friend of mine in one of the old-line churches read the part of this manuscript covering the intercessory power of the gift of tongues, then said, "Oral, won't there be problems with some who exercise the gift?" I said, "Let's face it, there will be problems but problems exist to be solved."

We would be less than honest to say there are no problems in using the gift of tongues. Of course, all these problems put together are not as serious as the ONE PROBLEM that exists where the gift of tongues (and interpretation) is not exercised at all! A woman once said to me, "I understand there are problems connected with tongues?" I replied, "There are problems connected with not exercising tongues too." Then I said, "The real problem is not with the gift of tongues. It has a valid and valuable ministry in behalf of believers. The problem is with a few people who attempt improperly to manifest this gift."

When you control your spirit, you can use wisdom in properly *timing* the exercising of your gift. Solomon said that there is a time to all things. There is a time to speak in tongues in your devotions, and a time to pray with your understanding. There is a time to exercise a gift of tongues in behalf of another or of a group, and there is a time to pray for them in your understanding. It's not an either/or, but a case of knowing where and when to speak, and where and when not to speak. It is a question of being in control of your emotions and simply using good judgment and common sense in harmony with the Word of God. It is exercising courtesy and respect for others who are used also to edify God's people. It is respect for other means such as prophecy, the preaching of God's Word, singing hymns, etc. It is being sensitive to the mood and moving of the Holy Spirit. It is being careful of timing the manifestation of the gift.

I recall how inspired I was the day the Spirit illumined my mind concerning Paul's statement in 1 Corinthians 14:37: "If any man think himself to be . . . spiritual, let him acknowledge that the things that I write unto you are the commandments of the Lord." This indicates spirituality is not only of moral conduct but also in obeying the rules laid down in God's Word for exercising the gifts of the Spirit. A helpful thing in knowing the rules is that it makes you bold to exercise your gift *fully*. You don't hold back for fear you will do wrong.

I am grateful that fresh insights are being given today. We know more about the gifts than ever before. Knowledge is increasing almost daily. I am reluctant to finish this book since I feel that by the time it is published God will have moved in me in a new dimension of power and knowledge and agape. I shared this thought with my good friend, William Pickthorn. He smiled and said, "Well, you can revise the book then and bring us up to date on what God shows you."

There is more fellowship and sharing going on today. Spirit-filled believers in both Pentecostal and historic churches are sitting down together in prayer groups, seminars, conventions. There is a hunger today for reality. Reality is Christ. It is the Holy Spirit who testifies of Christ in us.

Speaking in tongues helps release our inner being, through it we speak to our Saviour, we pray, we give thanks, we sing in the Spirit. Through this gift we experience a deepening of our love to God, our love for people and their salvation. We find a vitality of spirit and body that truly edifies us. "Every morning, my first greeting to my Lord is in tongues, then I greet Him with my understanding. It's like falling in love with Him anew every day," said a newly Spirit-filled believer to me recently. Another said, "I was never interested in the healing of the sick through prayer and faith until I was at a prayer group and received the infilling of the Holy Ghost. Gradually I developed a consciousness of the sick needing God's healing touch. Then one evening someone spoke a message in tongues and interpretation concerning the compassion of Jesus to heal. Now I ache to see the sick healed."

One of the nicest things happened in a prayer group which had asked me to share my concepts on healing. The meeting was in the home of a friend of mine and it was so packed that many had to sit on the floor. Nearing the intermission I noticed one of the young ladies seemed to be under a heavy anointing. I could tell she was striving almost desperately to exercise self-control. Our host and hostess had explained that the gifts were frequently manifested in their group, that they were welcomed and that they had been led to observe the rules laid down by Paul in 1 Corinthians 14. So the young lady would not permit herself to interrupt my talk no matter how much of the moving of the Spirit she felt. The very moment I ceased talking she reached her hand forth, touched me and said, "May I, please?" My wife who was seated next to me had sensed God wanted to give tongues and interpretation. As she caught my glance she was smiling and nodding her head. I said to the girl, "Please do." With her eyes closed and so quietly her voice was barely discernible through the room, she began to exercise a gift of tongues. It was a voice of beseeching at first, then it changed to a triumphant note. Just as quietly she gave the interpretation. God gave us a beautiful and powerful confirmation of the doctrine of healing. People left there that night knowing the Spirit had illuminated their minds and hearts to have compassion for the healing of the sick.

It was so cute the way she reached forth her hand, touched me and said, "May I, please?" Not only was she spiritual from the standpoint of contact with God, she was spiritual in keeping the rules in the exercising of the gift.

On the other hand, when one makes a habit of following a talk or sermon every time with tongues and interpretation it tends to focus attention on the gift and the person rather than on what God is saying. What such a person feels in such instances is usually an overflow of joy, a degree of the minister's burden, a stirring of his own spirit which does not necessarily mean he is to exercise a gift of tongues and interpretation. A talk or a sermon given by an anointed man or woman of God is sent straight from God to the understanding and heart of the hearer. Usually it needs no reinforcement. Leave it be. It will not return void, but will accomplish the purpose God has designed.

In this instance, one who feels moved to speak in tongues should do so quietly to himself and to God. In this way he will not distract from the deep impression made by God's Word and the faith that comes by hearing it spoken. A student at Stanford University where my son Ronnie was enrolled had become disturbed by utterances in tongues which broke the continuity of the service or interrupted the preaching of the Word and gave up speaking in tongues. He was afraid that if he allowed the gift to be exercised it would grow in him until he would become an interrupter too. Then suddenly he discovered that he could speak in tongues without moving his lips or uttering a sound; and he came to his pastor with great joy, saying, "Now I can be of real service during the preaching of the Word, for I can be used by the Spirit to help create an atmosphere of receptivity without interrupting the thought."

2. *Personal integrity.*

We read in Acts 6:3, "Wherefore, brethren, look ye out among you seven men of honest report, full of the Holy Ghost and wisdom, whom we may appoint over this business." Which comes first in this scripture, the honest report of the person chosen to be a ministering servant, or a manifestation of the Holy Ghost through him? It is honest report, isn't it? When one attempts to minister the power of the Holy Ghost in behalf of others, he is dealing with many lives, not merely his own. He may have all kinds of shortcomings and make many failures, but he must be honest. If he falls short in personal integrity, his witness will suffer. This is where sanctification is needed daily. There must be fruit of the Spirit corresponding to a ministry of the gifts of the Spirit.

When one speaks in tongues as a part of his own devotions,

he is seeking to edify himself. In exercising a gift of tongues, he is acting as a spokesman in behalf of other believers; for that moment, he is the center of interest. His personality is felt, also his spirit is dominant. What people feel coming from him is often as important as what he says. If they are convinced of his integrity they will respond in confidence, if not, they will react negatively.

On the other hand, the gift is given by the Spirit because He wills to do it (1 Corinthians 12:11), not because the believer is especially capable or worthy. Indeed, if this were not so, no one could qualify. When he endeavors to exercise his gift, he and the gift become one. The gift has integrity because it is from God. The believer must be worthy in character too, if he is to worthily manifest the gift. He must be able to produce fruit. He must be, in this sense, a good fruit tree. A tree with character produces good fruit. One without character or integrity will produce either scrawny fruit or nothing.

The Lord may not manifest a gift in us because of our worthiness but we have to be worthy in our character to exercise it effectively!

Paul indicates that one exercising a gift in a group of believers must submit himself to be judged. (1 Corinthians 14:29.) This virtually rules out a stranger passing through attempting to exercise tongues and interpretation. Why? Because the group does not know the kind of person he is, they are unable to judge him as to his manner of life and doctrine. Much of the abuse of tongues to which Paul refers in 1 Corinthians 14:19, 20, 33 and which has occurred in our day is by persons who are not qualified by knowledge or by a life of sanctification. They are unworthy in judgment and in character to minister in behalf of others. Paul said, "Know them which labour among you" (1 Thessalonians 5:12). This is another way of encouraging us to desire the manifestation of spiritual gifts in our midst and to know the believers ministering in our behalf. We can know them and we can boldly insist on worthiness in character and in knowledge of how to exercise the gift in an intelligent and profitable manner.

If we insist on the believer and his gift following the rules, or if we permit abuses, God holds us accountable either way. He knows that one or two abuses allowed to go uncorrected will bring confusion and discouragement, and that effective leadership by those in charge will inspire a more meaningful ministry of the gifts.

A pastor friend of mind, the Rev. Ralph Wilkerson, told how for weeks the gifts of the Spirit were operating profitably in his church. The needs of the people were being met. The church was growing and its influence was reaching far and wide. Then one night a stranger entered the meeting. In a loud voice, this individual attempted to give a message in tongues and interpretation. Instead of a hush falling over the group and their being able instantly to enter the mood of the Spirit, a spirit of confusion entered the service. The spirit of the person manifesting the gift was wrong. There was no love being manifested. Also the timing was wrong. At the close of the interpretation, this individual attempted to correct something in the group and to do it in a personal way. As the pastor related this episode, I asked him what he did. "At that moment," he replied, "I did not do anything. I did not want to pull up wheat with the tares, so when this individual finished, I changed the order of the service and proceeded to minister to the people."

Then he said, "However, when this individual came into our group the second time, I did do something."

I said, "What did you do?"

He said, "At the end of the meeting, I called this person into my office and read to her 1 Corinthians 14:27-33. I asked her if she were willing to be judged by the Word of God. She replied that the Spirit was guiding her and that she did not have to listen to me reading the Scripture to her. I then read verse 37: 'If any man think himself to be a prophet, or *spiritual*, let him acknowledge that the things that I write unto you are the commandments of the Lord.' I said to this person, 'If you are scriptural, you will acknowledge the rules that Paul laid down in the Scripture I have read to you. If not, you are not to attempt to manifest a gift in this church again.

You are welcome to attend and to have your needs met here, along with others. If you attempt to minister, you must come under the rules and responsibilities of those who are called to be ministers of the gospel.'

"This person replied, 'Then I will go where I can do what I want to do.' She has not been back to our services since." I pity the group where she is now unless she has become willing to obey the Word of God.

If a believer does not have an honest report, he must be encouraged to pay attention to his manner of day-by-day living. Perhaps he has overextended his credit or become negligent in fulfilling his commitments. He may have become careless in his speech or developed a selfishness that has become pronounced and apparent to the group. If he attempts, with this report of his life, to minister a gift of the Spirit in behalf of others, he may be sure that his sins will find him out.

Recently while reading Paul's epistles again, I was struck by the urgency with which he urged those who had become unworthy in character to repent. (2 Corinthians 7:9; 2 Timothy 2:25.) Sometimes I think repentance has become a lost ministry among God's people. Sin is taken so lightly that it is allowed to develop and become a terrible snare. Paul carried a tremendous burden that sin would be dealt with in his beloved brethren. When he received disquieting reports of uncorrected practices and unrepented sins among them, there was only one way to deal with such persons, and that was for them to repent. (2 Corinthians 12:20, 21.) The Apostle John was deeply concerned with this problem. He indicates that it is not he that *commits* sin who will be necessarily lost but he that *committeth* sin. It is the practice and pattern of sin that one allows to develop in his life that makes him of the devil and will ultimately destroy him. "He that committeth sin is of the devil" (1 John 3:8). On the other hand, John says, "If any man sin, we have an advocate with the Father, Jesus Christ the righteous" (1 John 2:1). He adds, "If we confess our sins, he is faithful and just to forgive us our sins, and to cleanse us from all [the practice and pattern] unrighteousness" (1 John 1:9).

8   Agape—*as Our Motivator*

Paul's closing statement in First Corinthians twelve, which is the chapter in which he talks about the nine gifts of the Spirit, concerns the way in which the gifts are to be manifested in us. "But covet earnestly the best gifts: and yet shew I unto you a more excellent way" (verse 31). Here he stresses the importance of the gifts. We are to "covet" them. Yet he says there is a more excellent way of desiring the gifts and that is through love. Not coveting but loving is the more excellent way. To covet means *ambitious desire*. To covet a gift out of our love for God and love for people is what the great Apostle is urging us to do.

To have a gift manifested through me is not to be *a badge of superiority*. It is to be a channel of loving ministry to meet the needs of people.

Paul's word in the Greek for love is *ágape*. It denotes a new quality of life, not a mere act or two of love. With agape we love like Christ loves; which is to love without regard to the quality or value of the object of our love. *Eros* or human love, loves because of the value of the object: "I love this person because. . . ." Agape is different: "I love this person in spite of. . . ."

Paul's entire teaching in 1 Corinthians 13 is based on agape. This opening statement in 1 Corinthians 14 is on agape. Because his emphasis is upon love, some have thought that Paul was actually condemning the manifestation of the gifts of the Spirit, particularly tongues and interpretation. This is not true and people are beginning to see it. He is simply putting things in their proper place so there can be a harmonious working of both agape and the gifts. In 1 Corinthians 14, the chapter in which he discusses tongues, interpretation and prophecy, he begins by saying, "Follow after charity [agape], and desire spiritual gifts." Our *desire* is for the Spirit to manifest gifts through us. Our *pursuit* in life is to be of agape so that whatever we seek to do with our gifts is to be motivated solely by God's love in our hearts.

The Rev. David du Plessis says, "A gift of the Spirit and love are like a train and a track. What is one without the other? You say you have a train? What about the track? If I say I have a gift, what about love? If I say I have love, what about the gift? Some say, 'You take the gift and I'll take love.' I say, 'I'll take both.' For what is love without a gift of the Spirit or the gift without love? Both are essential."

No gift can be successfully used without the person being motivated by love. Jesus said, "Ye shall receive power after that the Holy Ghost is come upon you: and ye shall be witnesses unto me" (Acts 1:8). He indicates that the highest purpose of the baptism with the Holy Ghost and the subsequent manifestation of any of the nine gifts of the Holy Ghost is to enable the believer to be an effective witness of Jesus, himself. As we have previously said, Jesus makes the believer himself the witness. Not only is he to bear witness, he *is* the witness. His witness is powerless (to reproduce Christ) without love.

Understanding 1 Corinthians 13

The essence of this great chapter is: let us be neither without love nor the gifts of the Spirit. Let us have both, love and gifts of the Spirit in proper balance. Some of the believers in Corinth had, to use an adage, "put the cart before the horse." Paul was not quarreling with what they had of the gifts of the Spirit but with how they were attempting to manifest these gifts. He was not against, say, their speaking in tongues. He spake in tongues himself and thanked God for speaking with tongues "more than ye all." (1 Corinthians 14:18.) He wished them to speak in tongues (1 Corinthians 14:5) and expressly told them not to forbid speaking in tongues. (1 Corinthians 14:39.)

Paul was not against prophecy. He said, "Ye may all prophesy" (1 Corinthians 14:31). He commended them that they did not "come behind in any gift" (1 Corinthians 1:7). His concern was with the motivation of their hearts in exercising these gifts. He ended chapter twelve by telling them there is a more excellent way for exercising the gifts than through coveting or ambitious desire. That more excellent way is through love, God's love. It's all right to "covet the best gifts" but it is better to be filled with love, for love not only attracts the gifts but provides the *climate*, and the *atmosphere* for their more effective use. (1 Corinthians 12:31.)

Comparison of Love and Gifts

The thirteenth chapter opens with Paul dramatically making his point by reversing the natural order in his approach to solving the problem.

To emphasize an important truth we often use a reverse illustration. A man says to his beloved wife, "Darling, if I should live to be a thousand years old I couldn't love you any more than I do now." He knows he can't possibly live to be that old in this life, she knows it too. She gets his meaning, however, he is declaring that he loves her with a whole heart.

It was in this area of meaning that Paul approaches the value God places on love as the motive for desiring spiritual gifts. The comparison he makes is not between the relative value of love over gifts or gifts over love. The comparison is between exercising gifts without love or exercising gifts with love.

Love must control the person through whom the Spirit manifests gifts. Without love the gifts are abused, without gifts love is too dormant.

Look at Paul's comparison: "Though I speak with the tongues of men and of angels, and have not charity, I am become as sounding brass, or a tinkling cymbal. And though I have the gift of prophecy, and understand all mysteries, and all knowledge; and though I have all faith, so that I could remove mountains, and have not charity, I am nothing. And though I bestow all my goods to feed the poor, and though

I give my body to be burned, and have not charity, it prof-iteth me nothing" (1 Corinthians 13:1-3).

Paul refers, (1) to speaking with the tongues of men and of angels, (2) to prophesying, divine knowledge and faith, and (3) to sacrifice and martyrdom . . . and compares their being done with love and their being done without love.

He uses strong language to emphasize a strong point.

Paul does not say, in these verses, that love is to go its separate way and the gifts to go their way. He does not say that either love or the gifts are superior to each other, nor that one is to be desired over the other. He says both love and the gifts are necessary to each other. Paul does not even say that the gifts are powerless without love. He suggests the possibility of the power of the gifts actually being released without love. Paul's point is that the *person* through whom gifts are manifested who is not motivated by love is (1) of no more value to himself than the sounding of the gongs of the heathen temples, (2) is profited nothing and (3) is nothing.

Paul's comparison of using the gifts without love is enough to shake the soul. He pictures a person doing mighty deeds through the gifts when the motivation is not love at all.

A person's daily walk with God profits him whereas his manifestation of gifts of the Spirit profits others. To help us have a daily walk of sanctification and holiness through which we grow the fruit of the Spirit, and to have a flowing of the power of the gifts to meet needs of people—that is the whole purpose of Paul's teaching in 1 Corinthians 12, 13 and 14. To have this walk in the Spirit is our reason for being.

The True Motivation

Paul refers to spiritual gifts being used, to charitable works being carried on, and to martyrdom being suffered. He says that the true motivation of these things is love, otherwise the person engaged in doing them is not profited in the sight of God and will end up as a nothing. That is strong language. For a person who does works of charity to be acceptable to God, he must do his works in agape love. This means that he loves *in spite of*, not *because of the value of*, the object. If his martyrdom is to be acceptable to God, the offering of his life must spring from a motive of God's love in his heart, otherwise his death leaves him without profit or value. The same is true of his exercising spiritual gifts. Paul says for the exercising of the gifts to be acceptable to God and to profit the person, he must be motivated by divine love. Exercising of the gifts might be profitable to others in helping them find deliverance; yet, if the motive is not agape, the exercising of these very spiritual gifts to help others will not be with profit to one's self.

It is asked, "Is it possible for one to exercise a gift of the Holy Spirit and profit others if he doesn't have God's love in his heart?" Paul indicates that this may happen both in the spiritual and non-spiritual realms. One might leave $1,000 to someone. Paul does not say this charitable gift will not aid the one who receives it, even if it is given without love. He says that the giver is profited nothing; because he lacks love he is nothing. But such a gift having as its source a heart of love blesses both giver and receiver alike. This is what God desires in both natural and supernatural things. Our motives must be examined daily to see that while we are blessing others that we shall not be unblessed ourselves.

One of the most tragic things in the world is for a person to exercise a gift of the Spirit such as the gift of faith, or the gift of working of miracles, or the gift of tongues, or the gift of prophecy, for instance, and be the instrument for meeting needs in people, and yet fail to profit himself because he lacks love. Paul reminds us that the giving of gifts "is to every man" (1 Corinthians 12:7) and they are the expression of divine love. For the gifts to profit both the one exercising them and those toward whom they are manifested, the person must give attention to love and the other fruit of the Spirit.

A Personal Experience

I remember once upon leaving a crusade service, a person followed me and kept insisting that I pray for his healing.

I had prayed for hundreds and was physically exhausted. All I could think of was to reach my room and get some rest. This person would not be denied, however, and I stopped and touched him for healing. Quite to my surprise he experienced healing. Why was I surprised that he had received help? You see I had touched him in anger. Anger because I felt I was being imposed on. How could he experience healing when I exercised the gift through anger, not love? Well, he was blessed but I was not. There was no elation in my heart as I went to my room. I felt I had failed God and myself by my irritation. The person went away rejoicing, I went away chagrined and disappointed in myself.

If I work on anything these days in myself, it is on my motive. Not only are we to have faith that the gifts will be manifested through us, we must strive to have more love, more gentleness and meekness, more longsuffering and other fruit of the Spirit. (Galatians 5:22, 23.)

We Must Grow Fruit

One of the fruit is temperance. I think we forget the enormous help we can receive from controlling our own spirit through temperance. (1 Corinthians 14:32.) Temperance or self-control is a fruit that would have aided me that evening when I touched my sick friend in anger. No matter how tired I was, or how much I felt I was a martyr to be asked to go the second mile; had I been working on temperance and self-control I could have touched him in love and received profit along with his blessing of healing. We both would have been profited.

Let us consider other characteristics of love as pointed out by Paul. "Charity suffereth long, and is kind; charity envieth not; charity vaunteth not itself, is not puffed up, doth not behave itself unseemly, seeketh not her own, is not easily provoked, thinketh no evil; rejoiceth not in iniquity, but rejoiceth in the truth; beareth all things, believeth all things, hopeth all things, endureth all things" (1 Corinthians 13:4-7).

Love is at the head of the list in the nine-fold fruit of the

Spirit. It is followed by joy, peace, longsuffering, gentleness, goodness, faith, meekness, temperance. Every one of these nine is to be working in us at all times, whereas the nine-fold *gifts* of the Spirit are distributed among the Body of Christ, in an individual member here and in one there. The entire nine gifts would scarcely be given to any individual, being "divided severally" as the Spirit wills. Paul says, "to one is given the word of wisdom, to another is given the word of knowledge," etc. The nine-fold fruit of the Spirit, however, is to be personally produced by the aid of the Spirit in each individual.

An individual may be given a gift of healing and may enjoy a free flow of its manifestation to heal the sick although he may be only one in the group in which the gift works. Not so with the fruit of the Spirit. All the fruit must be at work in him. I realize that Paul stressed the first of the fruit which is love; but, in 1 Corinthians 13:4-7, he points out that love is only complete if it has the quality of "suffering long." He describes love as having the attributes of the other fruit of the Spirit. In summing up these attributes we see that they are a repetition of the list in Galatians 5:22, 23, all summed up in the one word, agape.

Divine love is not listed as one of the nine gifts of the Spirit but it must be the motivation of the gifts. Love works no miracles without the gifts; and the gifts without love leave their possessor profitless. Love is the mightiest force of all, the force that is the superlative motive back of the gifts and sanctifying that desire. No wonder Paul begins the fourteenth chapter with: "Follow after love, and desire spiritual gifts."

I have said earlier in this book that when a gift of the Spirit is manifested through a believer, the manifestation is to meet needs in people and in that sense the believer becomes the messenger of the gift; he delivers it to the point of need where the gift meets the need and then, making a full circle, it returns to God the Holy Spirit. This is the way the gifts seem to do their work through me. More often than not the gift's manifestation comes very suddenly; and, all at once, I am aware that the gift has made its presence felt in me. As I minister under the power of the Spirit I am possessed with tremendous vigor and vitality. All my senses are alert, my mind is alive, my desire to help someone is intensified and I have a knowing that great things will be accomplished. Once the manifestation of the gifts subsides, I am keenly aware that I am reduced to a position of lesser power.

At this point what happens to the gift and where does it go? Is it not the property of the Spirit and returns to Him to await His bidding to be manifested through us at another time? Does it not make a full circle each time it is manifested? I realize this may not sound theologically correct but it is my experience, nevertheless, that it makes a full circle in each manifestation through me. This interpretation gives, in my opinion, greater glory to God and less to the individual. Instead of our appearing as some GREAT PERSON when the gift is manifested through us, we are seen as instruments of the Spirit with the greater glory going to Him.

It has always seemed a little disrespectful to hear someone saying, "I have a gift of ——." Isn't it better to say we are filled with the Spirit and from time to time He manifests a gift through us to meet the needs of the people?

I think this reasoning is in line with the third phase of love that Paul discusses in 1 Corinthians 13:8: "Charity never faileth: but whether there be prophecies, they shall fail; whether there be tongues, they shall cease; whether there be knowledge, it shall vanish away." First, Paul points out the absolute necessity of the gifts being exercised through the motivation of agape love. (1 Corinthians 13:1-3.) Next, he shows the characteristics of divine love to be characteristics of all the fruit of the Spirit. (1 Corinthians 13:4-7; Galatians 5:22, 23.) Here, in 1 Corinthians 13:8, we see the completion of the work of the gifts, making their full circle, while love continues forever.

Gifts Are Needed Today

The gifts are impermanent while love is eternal. First, Paul says, the day will come when prophecies, both of the gift of prophecy and the gift-inspired utterance of every believer, will fail to be needed. The reason for speaking in tongues will no longer exist and they will cease. At the same time the gift of knowledge, that divine insight and perception so necessary today, will vanish away. These three: prophecy, speaking in tongues and knowledge are by their nature impermanent, but still are essential for our work for God now.

"For we know in part, and we prophesy in part. But when that which is perfect is come, then that which is in part shall be done away. When I was a child, I spake as a child, I understood as a child, I thought as a child: but when I became a man, I put away childish things. For now we see through a glass, darkly; but then face to face: now I know in part; but then shall I know even as also I am known" (1 Corinthians 13:9-12).

When that which is permanent is come we will have no need for spiritual gifts, those divine aids for meeting the needs of the people. We need them now. They provide the power for us to fulfill our divine calling. When Christ, who is that which is Perfect, comes He will personally take over every part of our lives and as we behold Him face to face there will no longer be any need of spiritual gifts.

Even with the gifts working through us, what we do is only "in part," (verse 10). "For we know in part, and we prophesy in part," (verse 9). Ours is a fragment of the whole. What we have now is as much the supernatural workings of divine power as we shall have when Christ returns. In the here and now we are like a child growing up into a man. As a child leaves childhood when he becomes a man, so the gifts will be done away at Christ's coming. Paul states that as a child we think, understand and speak as a child—that is, as Christian believers we speak and understand and reason miraculously through the gifts of the Spirit as a Spirit-filled "child" of God.

May I remind you at this point that Paul wrote 1 Corinthians to believers who were baptized with the Holy Ghost and in actual possession of the gifts of the Spirit. He wrote to instruct them how to profitably use the gifts to meet the needs of people and edify the Body of Christ. Paul clearly stated that we "speak," "understand," "reason," "see through a glass darkly," "know in part," and are "as a child" before Christ's coming.

Here we are still developing, growing in the fruit of the Spirit, dependent upon the Spirit to manifest gifts through us. Here our normal measure of speech cannot compare with the perfect vocabulary of Jesus, our speaking with tongues in our prayers and praise toward God are not equal to our speaking to Him face to face and magnifying Him then in His Person. We are children here, half-developed, reaching forth toward maturity, praying, "Come, Lord Jesus" (Revelation 22:20). In this child-stage, we must have a manifestation of spiritual gifts through us as part of our supernatural equipment for service. Here we must be given a word of wisdom by the Spirit, or a word of knowledge by the same Spirit, or a gift of faith, or a gift of healing, or a gift of prophesy, or the gift of tongues and interpretation, etc.; but when we stand before our Lord and Saviour, our childhood needs will have their perfect answer and will be swallowed up in His glorious personal presence.

The gifts of the Spirit are all part of Christ and the Spirit takes of them and divides to us. (1 Corinthians 12:11.) Here we have fragments of His complete power, but then we have it full and complete. The fragment will "vanish away" but not before we embrace the whole in Christ's coming.

"And now abideth faith, hope, charity, these three; but the greatest of these is charity" (verse 13).

These three are eternal while the gifts are temporal. The blessed gifts of the Spirit are essential to us in exercising God's power to deliver people, but their use is for this life only. Faith, hope and love are not only for our Christian walk here, but they will abide forever. Their qualities are part of eternity. There will never be a time when they are not to be a part of us.

Love is the greatest, for love is what God is. Faith will endure forever, because our eternal relationship with God is based upon it. Hope will abide also for it is the outreach of faith into the infinite future.

9 The Companion Gift of Interpretation of Tongues

Paul indicates that the one exercising a gift of tongues may be praying well, or giving thanks well, but it is of NO VALUE TO OTHER BELIEVERS since they do not know the meaning of what is said to God in the Spirit. (1 Corinthians 14:16, 17.)

The other believers may feel in their spirit, and indeed they do, that something of a spiritual nature is being done in their behalf. Since, however, they can only understand through their intellect, God's response to the gift of tongues must be interpreted.

The gift of interpretation accomplishes a very important thing: it completes the intercessory ministry of the gift of tongues.

The gift of tongues has spoken to God in behalf of other believers, searching out inner weaknesses and needs, and linking them with the will of God and with the mind of the Spirit for them. The gift of interpretation gives God's *response* to the Spirit's intercession.

As I have pointed out, the gift of tongues interprets the believer's needs to God and the gift of interpretation interprets God's response to those needs. Notice that I use the term "God's response," rather than God's answer. *I do not wish to infer in any way that tongues are a cure-all for all our inner needs and problems. Very often, when one has spoken to God in tongues, and even received the interpretation, the problem or need still remains. The value of the gift of tongues is to have this need brought to God in a way that our intellect cannot. And the value of interpretation of tongues is to bring back to our understanding what is the will of God and the mind of the Spirit concerning it.*

Tongues and interpretation are divine communications to

God and from God to the Church. We speak to Him "in the Spirit" and He speaks to us by the Spirit "in our understanding." (1 Corinthians 14:2, 15, 16.) As we talk to God through tongues and He talks to us through interpretation; we gain inspiration and understanding; we feel His presence and gain strength; we begin better to learn what is in the mind of His Spirit for us.

How does this come about? Paul explains it in 1 Corinthians 14:5, 6: "I would that ye all spake with tongues, but rather that ye prophesied: for greater is he that prophesieth than he that speaketh with tongues, except he interpret, that the church may receive edifying. Now, brethren, if I come unto you speaking with tongues, what shall I profit you, except I shall speak to you either by revelation, or by knowledge, or by prophesying, or by doctrine?"

THE GIFT MUST EDIFY OTHERS

Notice in verse 5 that Paul refers to the gift of tongues which is for the edifying of the Church or a group of believers. To edify the Church, the gift of tongues has to reach God since God alone can strengthen and build us up in our inner man. The end of this gift is *edification*. Here Paul states that a believer who exercises a gift of tongues is as valuable to meeting the needs of the Church as one who gives a prophecy, providing he also interprets God's response to tongues to the people. If he interprets, his contribution to the edifying of the Church is on equal par with that of one who contributes a prophetic utterance. The Spirit uses him to minister in behalf of the people. This is one of the reasons Paul emphasizes divine love in 1 Corinthians 13. Without love, this believer, however well he may exercise his gift is not benefited and becomes as nothing. As he ministers his gift of love, not only are the people benefited but he is blessed as well. *The emphasis Paul places upon love indicates that what people feel from us while we are ministering is as important as what they hear from our tongue.*

At one time we thought that tongues plus interpretation

equaled prophecy. This is not what Paul said at all. What he says is that the believer who exercises the gift of tongues and also interprets, is placed on an equal footing with one who prophesies. Yet while interpretation and prophecy are related, they are not the same. Prophecy may become a part of a message in tongues, but prophecy can also be an inspired utterance having no connection with tongues.

Verse 6 of chapter 14 shows the combination of the gift of tongues and interpretation being used to edify a group of believers. Paul completes his thought in verse 5—where he referred to tongues and interpretation being as valuable as a prophecy—by saying, "Now, brethren, if I come unto you speaking with tongues, what shall I profit you EXCEPT. . . ." Here he pauses. "Except," suggests there is something else to be added. "Except, I shall speak to you (through interpretation) either by revelation, or by knowledge, or by prophesying, or by doctrine?" With my added parenthesis, I think you can get the sense of Paul's meaning.

Paul wants us to see that the gift of tongues cannot function alone. In this sense, tongues and interpretation are the gifts of the Spirit that cannot operate more or less independently of each other. While all the gifts have some interaction and interlocking, any of the first seven—word of wisdom, word of knowledge, faith, gifts of healing, working of miracles, prophecy, and discerning of spirits—can be manifested as a separate entity. For example, if the gift of healing is manifested in me, it can perform independently of any of the other gifts. This is not true with the gift of tongues and interpretation of tongues. It takes the gift of interpretation to make the gift of tongues valid, meaningful, and complete to the Body of Christ.

HOW DOES INTERPRETATION COMPLETE THE GIFT OF TONGUES?

Paul speaks of at least four responses that God makes through the gift of interpretation to complete the ministry of the gift of tongues and to activate other gifts of the Spirit. These are *revelation, knowledge, prophecy* and *doctrine.* (1 Corinthians 14:6.)

1. By revelation.

In November 1962, when I was installed by the Board of Regents as president of our University, Demos Shakarian, one of the members of our Board of Trustees, spoke through the gift of tongues. It was a fluent language and as we listened, we felt God's presence as though it were quite tangible in the room. When Demos ceased speaking, someone started to interpret, when immediately Demos sensed he had spoken to God in my behalf, and that the Spirit would reveal to me what the meaning was. Instantly the interpretation was given inside me: *I was to be given a new dimension of the Holy Spirit and I was to have it all the days of my life.* This was the one thing I desired that day more than anything else. In launching a great University where thousands of youth would come to study from all over the world, I had felt that the very essence of the healing ministry should become a valid part of our training program. These youth would receive not only a fine academic education, but would become witnesses unto Jesus Christ through whatever career they chose to follow.

I knew too that God was leading me to continue my evangelistic ministry, and that the University was to become another one of our world outreaches. Never will I forget the impact of that revelation. Never will I forget the edification I felt that hour as the Holy Ghost revealed how completely He would possess me and that in this way He would use me as His minister as long as I should live.

Revelation can take several different forms, each one bringing spiritual illumination to our understanding. Recently there was another manifestation through tongues and interpretation regarding our ministry. (I am giving you these personal experiences to illustrate the point we are endeavoring to make.) While praying with a group, God moved upon one of the believers who prayed through the gift of tongues. The interpretation followed: "I have reserved a portion of My power that has not yet been given; now I will reveal it." This was followed by another manifestation of tongues and interpretation. We had been discussing how we could win more souls, particularly in reference to bringing students to the University from all over the world. I had felt for years that God was going to do these things and that the University was to become part of His larger purpose of helping us witness to all mankind. The second interpretation, "I am doing what I told you I would do," was a revelation to me, confirming God's leading in my life that I was on the right track and we were on schedule. The revelation, "I have reserved a portion of My power that has not yet been given: now I will reveal it," was another confirmation of something that I had deeply believed would come to pass. It is thrilling to know that we will be given more of God's power to meet the needs of people as we near the coming of Christ.

2. By knowledge.

The gift of interpretation, like the gift of prophecy, is a communicative gift. It is conveying something to the understanding of the believer or the Church. It often makes use of the gift of the word of knowledge to accomplish this.

When Paul spoke of the four ways that interpretation completes the ministry of the gift of tongues, he included knowledge. This would be a word of knowledge which is the second of the nine gifts of the Spirit and which brings divine insight and perception. (1 Corinthians 12:8.) There are times when an entire church group is baffled by a situation, they cannot understand it at all. It continues to perplex and hinder them. Eventually it reaches a state that not even the preaching of the Word of God by an anointed minister can solve. The communicative gift of the word of knowledge as it functions alone or in the gift of interpretation becomes God's instrument to bring understanding and help concerning this situation to the minds of the believers. In this particular instance, the gift of tongues interprets this perplexing situation to God in behalf of the believers. Interpretation follows to illumine the minds of the believers concerning what is the mind of the Spirit concerning it. The gift of tongues gathers it up and supernaturally speaks it to God, and the interpretation reveals a word of knowledge concerning it.

3. By prophesying.

As we know, the gift of prophecy can operate without being joined to any other of the nine gifts. However, Paul points out that it sometimes works in conjunction with tongues and interpretation. The interpretation includes a prophecy which is brought to bear upon the critical situation facing the believers. As we see in Paul's teaching on prophecy, prophecy goes beyond the edification function of tongues to include exhortation and comfort. (1 Corinthians 14:3.)

Here, interpretation includes a prophecy conveying an exhortation to the people from God. It is a message straight from God. These prophecies or exhortations are not to be despised. Paul says in 1 Thessalonians 5:20, "Despise not prophesying," God really speaks to those believers who will listen. Prophecy, both as a gift and as a part of interpretation of tongues, was a common occurrence in the assemblies of the Early Church. Believers were urged, "Covet to prophesy" (1 Corinthians 14:39). However it is wise to remember that the same rules governing an exercise of gifts of tongues and interpretation apply to the gift of prophecy, as well.

Prophesying through interpretation of tongues is limited to exhorting and comforting, not for guidance. (1 Corinthians 14:3.) Guidance is not listed as one of its functions, as indeed it is not the function of any of the gifts of the Spirit, nor does it take the place of good common sense, balanced judgment, and the Word of God.

The interpretive form of prophesying exhorts to action but does not "lead." In the Early Church, prophecy predicted things that would come to pass but left the "leadings" to the prerogative and judgment of the believer concerned. (Acts 11:28; 21:10.)

I am pointing this out because of the fact that no matter how a gift of the Spirit may be manifested through a believer, he is still a human being and needs improvement. It is a beautiful and powerful thing when one is exercising the gift of interpretation of tongues and gives a prophecy or exhortation, especially when he leaves the results with God. On the other hand, one's zeal can run beyond his knowledge and he can go beyond what the Spirit seeks to do through him. If he does not use wisdom, he can follow his exhortation with a spirit of attempting to correct and rebuke which normally comes through the Word of God and the anointed preaching of God's Word. Even when Paul was distressed over the abuses in the Corinthian Church concerning Holy Communion, tongues and interpretation, prophecy, lack of love, and other things, he used words of helpfulness and encouragement. He exhorted them, but did not condemn them to judgment and hell. The gentle exhortation that is a part of tongues and interpretation is a real inspiration to the believers to come closer to God and to cast all their care upon Him and to trust Him.

Comfort! What a blessed word. "Then had the churches rest throughout all Judæa and Galilee and Samaria, and were edified; and walking in the fear of the Lord, and in the comfort of the Holy Ghost, were multiplied" (Acts 9:31). Through tongues and interpretation, God's people can really be comforted.

4. By doctrine.

Phillips' translation gives "doctrine" as: *some teaching about the Christian life.*

Paul teaches us that doctrine is important. We learn the doctrine of God as we study His Word and hear His Word preached and taught by God-anointed men and women. (Ephesians 4:11, 13.) It is difficult for man to grasp true doctrine by his intellect alone. There is so much of God that can be grasped only by the Spirit. At times, through tongues and interpretation, a doctrine will be illuminated and will stand out in the thoughts of the believers so that it can assume its proper place of importance in their thinking and believing. Though even this must be in harmony with the Word of God.

10 Rules for Interpretation of Tongues

Interpretation of tongues is done by a believer filled with the Holy Spirit who is sensitive to the Spirit and to the needs of other believers. The believer, either man or woman, is one known to the group, a member in good standing and who exercises the gift in a responsible manner. His ministry is public in the sense that it is before the group. It is brief, lasting usually only seconds or a few minutes. He functions after a gift of tongues has been exercised and completes its ministry to the group. Both gifts of tongues AND interpretation may be manifested through him. There are definite goals for interpreting effectively.

1. Pray to interpret.

The ability to interpret is generously promised if we pray for it. "Wherefore let him that speaketh in an unknown tongue pray that he may interpret" (1 Corinthians 14:13). Insist on this ability, Paul did. (1 Corinthians 14:27, 28.) Through interpretation a fuller and freer use of tongues is possible, putting tongues in their rightful place instead of restricting their use or prohibiting them. According to Paul, tongues are not to be forbidden. They are of necessity restricted, however, when no interpreter is present to explain the meaning of God's response to a gift of tongues. At such times, the one exercising the gift of tongues may continue despite the lack of an interpreter AS LONG AS HE SPEAKS TO HIMSELF AND TO GOD. (1 Corinthians 14:28.)

The problem in the Corinthian Church was not the gift of tongues as much as it was a lack of interpreters. Throughout the fourteenth chapter Paul pleads for and insists on interpreters so that the gift of tongues might edify the Church.

How much we miss when the gift of tongues is not followed immediately by the inspired utterance of interpretation. In that instance, the speaker in tongues must restrict himself and reduce his gift to simple tongues and speak quietly to himself and to God. Anything that is restricted is not free! Anything reduced is not growing! No wonder Paul urged, "Pray that ye may interpret."

2. *Know you have the interpretation first.*

The Holy Spirit divides this gift, like He does the others, as He wills. (1 Corinthians 12:11.) You cannot become an interpreter in a public way unless the Spirit gives you the ability. The interpretation is God's response to the gift of tongues, the content is inspired. It does not originate in your intellect, even as tongues do not. Interpretation may pass *through* your intellect, but it originates in the Holy Spirit. Therefore you can interpret only when it is given you.

How can you know? And how do you interpret?

A. The interpretation may suddenly appear, in its entirety, in your mind. You can see it like on the pages of a book.

B. You may be given only the sense of it before you speak.

C. You may be given the first few words only before you begin.

D. There will be a *knowing* within you. You may momentarily experience a degree of normal human reluctance or fright but it will not be a fear. The inner knowing will cancel out any fear.

The interpretation will not be the same each time you interpret. The gift of tongues includes "divers kinds of tongues." It goes from need to need in its intercessory ministry. Your interpretation must be true to God's response to those needs brought before Him by the gift of tongues.

You will want to be careful not to fall into copying some other interpreter. The use of archaic words such as *thou* and *thee* are not necessary at all. Since you are interpreting and explaining God's response, you may use words ordinarily employed in your normal speech.

Another thing that is wise to avoid is not to begin the interpretation with: Thus saith the Lord. The interpreter is doing the interpreting, not God. When he attempts to interpret as if God Himself was speaking every word, he is putting an awful strain upon himself. Since the interpreter is human and therefore not perfect, he is assuming a serious risk when he attempts to begin his utterance with: Thus saith the Lord. It is usually wiser to simply give God's response without prefacing it with such phrases. Do not fear that this will lessen the effect of the utterance. Any utterance that is inspired of God will hold an audience. The more humble and unassuming one can be, and at the same time be positive, the more effective he will be.

3. Speak in a normal voice.

Remember you are addressing the words of God's *response* to other believers, speaking to their *understanding*, not their *emotions*. Anytime you use your emotions or your voice in a way that calls attention to you rather than to the inspired utterance you are endeavoring to give, the less effective you will be as Christ's witness in that hour.

Remember, too, your interpretation takes one or more of four forms: revelation, word of knowledge, prophecy, doctrine. (1 Corinthians 14:6.) Simply speak in a voice loud enough to be heard, and be your normal self as much as possible. Seek to get the group to notice what you are saying rather than the way you say it.

Any time the interpreter shouts out or yells or screams, he needs to remind himself of the scriptural injunction to control his spirit. Emotion for emotion's sake will ruin the effect of the message and spoil the interpreter's witness.

4. Stop when the interpretation is finished.

Sometimes the interpretation may be a longer utterance

than the time used in manifesting the gift of tongues. The interpreter, in giving God's response, is given to the understanding and may require more words to convey the full meaning. Whether the response is long or short depends on the Holy Spirit, not the interpreter. The interpreter should resist any desire to embellish the message he is giving. He should be careful not to over-involve his intellect in it. The interpretation may take five words or a few hundred.

An old-timer, wise in the use of tongues and interpretation, has said, "The interpreter should speak up, shut up and let the message of the Spirit center itself on Jesus Christ to meet the needs of the believers." I agree wholeheartedly.

5. *Be willing to be judged.*

Paul says, "Let the prophets speak two or three, and let the other judge" (1 Corinthians 14:29). We have said before that anyone exercising a gift of the Spirit becomes in that exercise a ministering servant. He may be a preacher or he may be an ordinary layman.

In the same way that a preacher is judged as to ability to preach, sensitivity to God and the people, conducting himself honorably and responsibly, being motivated by love, having faith, etc., so a layman who exercises a gift of the Spirit is to be judged in the same way. If he is willing to be judged, God can use him with his gift; if not, he can frustrate God's purposes as well as frustrate himself.

The judging is to be done by those believers who also exercise gifts of the Spirit. "And let the other(s) judge." The interpreter is to be judged on the honest report of his character, his timing in utterance, his utterance being in harmony with the Word of God, and on whether the result of his utterance edifies, causes others to learn, and receive comfort.

6. *Be in control of your spirit.*

Any exercising of a gift of the Spirit is a divine-human reciprocity. It is an interaction of God and the believer. Part is on a natural base, part is based on the supernatural. God is infallible, the believer is not. Rules are laid down to assist the believer to do the very best he can to exercise his gift worthily. Then he is urged by Paul to remain in control of his spirit.

The interpreter may "feel" the thrill of the move of the Spirit within him. Excitement may grip him so that he would like to jump up and down, to yell at the top of his voice. That isn't his mission. He is to interpret, not indulge in gymnastics. Others are hushed and waiting, their needs have been illumined before God, God's response is about to be revealed. They can get the response only through their understanding. The interpreter, in control of himself, can now speak calmly and be a real blessing to those present.

7. *Try to know the measure of your faith.*

"Having gifts (faculties, talents, qualities) that differ according to the grace given us, let us use them: [He whose gift is] prophecy, [let him prophesy] according to the proportion of his faith" (Romans 12:6 Amplified Version). Paul indicates there are varying degrees of faith. That is faith that flows out in action, faith that is released. There is a maximum and a minimum, indicating that when one exercises a gift of the Spirit, which in this case is the interpretation of tongues, he is to minister up to the maximum of his faith. He is not to fall short of the top level.

In other words, when one receives an interpretation he is to respond positively, to exercise the gift boldly and confidently, and to allow the joy of the Lord to flow through him.

8. *Value God's Word.*

The preacher is under Christ's command to "preach the Word" which is said to be "sharper than a two-edged sword." When preached, God's Word produces faith. "Faith cometh by hearing." The Word is central in our worship of God whether we are alone in our private devotions or in a public service in the church. Our Christian experience and walk in the Spirit are based on it.

On the other hand, tongues are a devotional experience wherein the believer's spirit prays and gives thanks "in the Spirit." It is still a devotional experience in its gift-form, and is exercised in behalf of the needs of believers. Through interpretation, tongues bring revelation, word of knowledge, prophecy, and doctrine to edify the Body of Christ. But—and this is important to know—tongues and interpretation are not a *guide*. The revelation, or the word of knowledge, or the prophecy, or the doctrine brought by the inspired utterances of tongues and interpretation are given to "help." They cannot act as a substitute for the preaching of God's Word and the study of it. They cannot be given independently of the teachings of the Holy Scriptures. They help edify and comfort us, they illumine the teachings of the Word, and they bring fresh new insights into the walk in the Spirit. We need them and can have them and are beginning, in a growing manner, to have them. We must be careful to maintain the proper balance between *what is written* and *what is being revealed* at the moment through the gifts of the Spirit. It is not that God would manifest a gift that is not in harmony with the general teaching of His written Word. Not that at all. It is the human tendency to err that we are to watch.

"Beloved, believe not every spirit, but try the spirits whether they are of God. . . . Hereby know ye the Spirit of God: Every spirit that confesseth that Jesus Christ is come in the flesh is of God" (1 John 4:1, 2). This is the measuring stick; the spirit of anyone attempting to exercise a gift centers his emphasis on Jesus Christ, the Son of God. Jesus said that when the Holy Ghost is come, "He shall testify of me" (John 15:26). At the center of every interpretation that is truly inspired by the Holy Spirit is God's Son, Jesus Christ. Further, the whole tenor of the interpretation is in perfect harmony with the full teaching of the written Word of God.

The fact that we are told to "try the spirits" to see if they are of God, points up human frailty and error. I once heard a layman who both exercises the gifts of the Spirit and thoroughly knows the Word say to another believer whose interpretation did not quite harmonize with the general teachings of the Scriptures. "You did not receive your prophecy clearly. You let your own spirit and imagination enter in. If you intend to be used of the Lord like this, I suggest you also study His Word so you can keep balanced." It is encouraging to see laymen take this stand. It means God will manifest His gifts through all of us more in the future.

Everything is right with tongues and interpretation when the believer is right. He is the one who makes this exercise valid, or out of place.

9. Don't monopolize.

When an interpreter monopolizes, he becomes competitive and is heading for trouble. Paul states, "If any man speak in an unknown tongue, let it be by two, or at the most by three, and that by course; and let one interpret" (1 Corinthians 14:27). The Amplified Version gives this verse: "If some speak in a [strange] tongue, let the number be limited to two or at the most three, and each one [taking his] turn, and let one interpret and explain [what is said]."

The number exercising tongues and interpretation in a group is limited to two or three, each one is to take his turn, and one is to interpret and explain what is said. *Sometimes the interpreter explains what is said* TO GOD *in tongues, so that the group may enter into the Spirit's intercession in their behalf*. I have seen this bring real edification. Of course, the response of God to the mysteries uttered by tongues, is the principal thing that must enter the understanding of those present.

It is usually best for one person to interpret. Ordinarily one person can get all the meaning of one manifestation of the gift of tongues. Several interpreters may get the identical interpretation at the same time. One, however, can give the meaning of God's response. And even as two or three believers are allowed to exercise the gift of tongues in one meeting, one at a time and in rotation, so logically it follows there could be more than one interpreter functioning, too.

The interpreter will want to wait and see if God will use another. A professor of medicine at one of the large universities has recently been filled with the Spirit. He finds he can interpret readily. He finds also he can wait for others and still give the interpretation if it has not been given perfectly. He even encourages others to pray for this ability, and to give part or all of an interpretation from time to time. You can imagine how he is loved and respected in his group.

This points up another thing. An interpreter who waits and gives way to another should be sure the right interpretation is given. If a false note is injected by someone who "thinks he is interpreting" but really is not, the proven interpreter should kindly but definitely point out the error and give the true interpretation.

10. Grow fruit of the Spirit to match the exercising of your gift.

These are goals toward which we strive. At the same time we realize that the Spirit is using earthen vessels, and He is using us while we are growing and maturing. If this were not so, we could never have the courage and honesty to attempt exercising any gift of the Spirit. We would look at our unworthiness and give up.

The possibility of growing fruit of the Spirit is very real. We are encouraged to grow, to walk in the Spirit. (Galatians 5:22, 23.) Paul tells us to "follow after love" (1 Corinthians 14:1). The fruit of joy can be ours, too. The Word says, "The joy of the Lord is your strength."

In Hong Kong once the Spirit spoke to my heart about joy. "If you will seek My joy . . . I will give you souls." When joy fills me, I feel strength. *Peace* is another fruit. *Longsuffering, goodness, faith, gentleness, meekness, temperance* complete the list. They are all expressions of love. If we can really love, God can really use us.

11 The Place of God's Word in Exercising a Gift of Tongues and Interpretation

It is significant and pertinent to the issues today, and to us who appreciate tongues and interpretation, that there is only one area where Paul diminishes the value of tongues. He refers to it in 1 Corinthians 14:19, "Yet in the church I had rather speak five words with my understanding, that by my voice I might teach others also, than ten thousand words in an unknown tongue."

The situation existed when (1) Paul was in church, (2) when he was teaching others in the church service, and (3) when he was trying to reach the hearers with God's Word through their understanding. He had discovered through practical experience that when he was teaching or preaching, five words spoken through his understanding (not through his spirit) were more effective than ten thousand words in tongues. No one can accuse Paul of being against speaking in tongues nor of not appreciating the privilege to speak to God "in the Spirit." In the preceding verse, verse 18, he said, "I thank my God I speak with tongues more than ye all." He indicates tongues were a valid and frequent part of his devotions to God, but as an instrument of teaching and preaching, tongues are virtually without value. Their purpose is not to teach or to preach but to be spoken TO GOD to bring edification. Tongues do not come through the understanding either of the one speaking or of those listening. When you consider five words worth more than ten thousand, you begin to see that when one teaches he uses his understanding to put the teaching in words that others can understand.

Perfectly sincere people can violate Paul's rule and think that they are in divine order. Two things are apparent: either they don't know God's Word concerning the gift of tongues, or they are not in control of their own spirit—or both. When this is true, there is always the risk for such a person to speak out of turn in a public meeting. On a few occasions this has occurred in our crusades when thousands were gathered to hear the Word of God preached and receive salvation and healing. I recall one evening on the West Coast when nearly ten thousand were present and I was bringing the sermon to a close and in the act of inviting the unsaved to come forward and accept Christ as their personal Saviour. Suddenly the meeting was interrupted by a perfectly sincere woman who felt the urge to speak in tongues. Since the crowd was so large and one could not be heard without a public-address system, all we could hear was a volume of strange words. It made no sense at all to the audience, many of whom knew nothing about speaking in tongues in the first place. Their attention was diverted and the sense of the altar call was lost. Less than half of the several hundred who usually come forward did so. It was heartbreaking.

Am I discouraged by such interruptions? Not at all. I think they are terribly out of place, but they do not cancel out the valid use of the gift of tongues. Paul did not condone such abuses of tongues, neither do I or other responsible spiritual men and women. Paul did not like abuses of the Holy Communion either, but he didn't order it to cease or to be forbidden. Instead he gave clear directions concerning it. (1 Corinthians 11:20-34.)

In dealing with tongues, you and I, like Paul, can be a part of the answer, instead of being a part of the problem. What is the answer? It is certainly not in forbidding tongues. To forbid is to violate Paul's command in 1 Corinthians 14:39. One leader said, "It is better to have a little wild fire than no fire at all." It has been rightly said, "There is nothing wrong with tongues when the person is right." He is right when he exercises his gift according to Paul's rules in 1 Corinthians 14: by being *in control of his spirit, carefully timing his utterance; by not using tongues to reach people's understanding;* and, if he feels he has to speak in tongues while God's

Word is being taught in a public assembly, to do so *quietly to himself and to God*.

Through more than 27 years of bringing the gospel to crowds ranging from tens to tens of thousands, I have yet to see a substitute for the preaching and teaching of the Word of God; not tongues, not hymns, not entertainment, not anything! God's Word is central and indispensable. "Faith cometh by hearing and hearing by the word of God" (Romans 10:17). We value God's Holy Word both in and out of the public assembly!

This does not rule out tongues and interpretation in their proper place. There are occasions when the Spirit will shed light on a subject or reveal a response from God through these gifts. This is seldom in a mixed audience; usually it is in a smaller group when those present understand the purpose of tongues. I am reminded of a layman's seminar at our School of Evangelism (a division of Oral Roberts University), that just as I finished a talk on the *Gifts of the Spirit* there was a message in tongues and interpretation. At first it seemed I was being interrupted in my teaching. The group grew uneasy but it was not as it appeared. (1) I was dealing with a group of believers, and (2) I had finished, although they were not completely aware of this fact. This believer spoke in tongues, interpreted and immediately walked forward and asked to be judged. We were delighted. She was in order, her timing was correct (I had finished and was waiting on the Spirit to give further guidance), what she said through interpretation illuminated what I had taught, and she was humble and full of love.

However, I wish to point out that sometimes the Holy Spirit acts sovereignly. We must learn that we must not allow ourselves to stereotype Him. At such times the spiritual ones know it is God moving. On rare occasions, He will manifest a gift of tongues and interpretation, seemingly in a way that is not in accordance with the broad general rules laid down in the Scripture. At the same time, He never contradicts Himself or does violence to His Word. The Holy Spirit is a perfect gentleman. We can trust Him.